Hinduism: A Very Short Introduction

VERY SHORT INTRODUCTIONS are for anyone wanting a stimulating and accessible way into a new subject. They are written by experts, and have been translated into more than 40 different languages.

The series began in 1995, and now covers a wide variety of topics in every discipline. The VSI library now contains over 450 volumes—a Very Short Introduction to everything from Psychology and Philosophy of Science to American History and Relativity—and continues to grow in every subject area.

Very Short Introductions available now:

ACCOUNTING Christopher Nobes
ADVERTISING Winston Fletcher
AFRICAN AMERICAN RELIGION Eddie S. Glaude Jr.
AFRICAN HISTORY John Parker and Richard Rathbone
AFRICAN RELIGIONS Jacob K. Olupona
AGNOSTICISM Robin Le Poidevin
ALEXANDER THE GREAT Hugh Bowden
ALGEBRA Peter M. Higgins
AMERICAN HISTORY Paul S. Boyer
AMERICAN IMMIGRATION David A. Gerber
AMERICAN LEGAL HISTORY G. Edward White
AMERICAN POLITICAL HISTORY Donald Critchlow
AMERICAN POLITICAL PARTIES AND ELECTIONS L. Sandy Maisel
AMERICAN POLITICS Richard M. Valelly
THE AMERICAN PRESIDENCY Charles O. Jones
THE AMERICAN REVOLUTION Robert J. Allison
AMERICAN SLAVERY Heather Andrea Williams
THE AMERICAN WEST Stephen Aron
AMERICAN WOMEN'S HISTORY Susan Ware
ANAESTHESIA Aidan O'Donnell
ANARCHISM Colin Ward
ANCIENT ASSYRIA Karen Radner
ANCIENT EGYPT Ian Shaw
ANCIENT EGYPTIAN ART AND ARCHITECTURE Christina Riggs
ANCIENT GREECE Paul Cartledge
THE ANCIENT NEAR EAST Amanda H. Podany
ANCIENT PHILOSOPHY Julia Annas
ANCIENT WARFARE Harry Sidebottom
ANGELS David Albert Jones
ANGLICANISM Mark Chapman
THE ANGLO-SAXON AGE John Blair
THE ANIMAL KINGDOM Peter Holland
ANIMAL RIGHTS David DeGrazia
THE ANTARCTIC Klaus Dodds
ANTISEMITISM Steven Beller
ANXIETY Daniel Freeman and Jason Freeman
THE APOCRYPHAL GOSPELS Paul Foster
ARCHAEOLOGY Paul Bahn
ARCHITECTURE Andrew Ballantyne
ARISTOCRACY William Doyle
ARISTOTLE Jonathan Barnes
ART HISTORY Dana Arnold
ART THEORY Cynthia Freeland
ASTROBIOLOGY David C. Catling
ATHEISM Julian Baggini
AUGUSTINE Henry Chadwick
AUSTRALIA Kenneth Morgan
AUTISM Uta Frith
THE AVANT GARDE David Cottington
THE AZTECS David Carrasco
BACTERIA Sebastian G. B. Amyes
BARTHES Jonathan Culler
THE BEATS David Sterritt
BEAUTY Roger Scruton
BESTSELLERS John Sutherland

THE BIBLE John Riches
BIBLICAL ARCHAEOLOGY Eric H. Cline
BIOGRAPHY Hermione Lee
BLACK HOLES Katherine Blundell
THE BLUES Elijah Wald
THE BODY Chris Shilling
THE BOOK OF MORMON Terryl Givens
BORDERS Alexander C. Diener and Joshua Hagen
THE BRAIN Michael O'Shea
THE BRITISH CONSTITUTION Martin Loughlin
THE BRITISH EMPIRE Ashley Jackson
BRITISH POLITICS Anthony Wright
BUDDHA Michael Carrithers
BUDDHISM Damien Keown
BUDDHIST ETHICS Damien Keown
BYZANTIUM Peter Sarris
CANCER Nicholas James
CAPITALISM James Fulcher
CATHOLICISM Gerald O'Collins
CAUSATION Stephen Mumford and Rani Lill Anjum
THE CELL Terence Allen and Graham Cowling
THE CELTS Barry Cunliffe
CHAOS Leonard Smith
CHEMISTRY Peter Atkins
CHILD PSYCHOLOGY Usha Goswami
CHILDREN'S LITERATURE Kimberley Reynolds
CHINESE LITERATURE Sabina Knight
CHOICE THEORY Michael Allingham
CHRISTIAN ART Beth Williamson
CHRISTIAN ETHICS D. Stephen Long
CHRISTIANITY Linda Woodhead
CITIZENSHIP Richard Bellamy
CIVIL ENGINEERING David Muir Wood
CLASSICAL LITERATURE William Allan
CLASSICAL MYTHOLOGY Helen Morales
CLASSICS Mary Beard and John Henderson
CLAUSEWITZ Michael Howard
CLIMATE Mark Maslin
CLIMATE CHANGE Mark Maslin
THE COLD WAR Robert McMahon
COLONIAL AMERICA Alan Taylor
COLONIAL LATIN AMERICAN LITERATURE Rolena Adorno
COMEDY Matthew Bevis
COMMUNISM Leslie Holmes
COMPLEXITY John H. Holland
THE COMPUTER Darrel Ince
CONFUCIANISM Daniel K. Gardner
THE CONQUISTADORS Matthew Restall and Felipe Fernández-Armesto
CONSCIENCE Paul Strohm
CONSCIOUSNESS Susan Blackmore
CONTEMPORARY ART Julian Stallabrass
CONTEMPORARY FICTION Robert Eaglestone
CONTINENTAL PHILOSOPHY Simon Critchley
CORAL REEFS Charles Sheppard
CORPORATE SOCIAL RESPONSIBILITY Jeremy Moon
CORRUPTION Leslie Holmes
COSMOLOGY Peter Coles
CRIME FICTION Richard Bradford
CRIMINAL JUSTICE Julian V. Roberts
CRITICAL THEORY Stephen Eric Bronner
THE CRUSADES Christopher Tyerman
CRYPTOGRAPHY Fred Piper and Sean Murphy
THE CULTURAL REVOLUTION Richard Curt Kraus
DADA AND SURREALISM David Hopkins
DANTE Peter Hainsworth and David Robey
DARWIN Jonathan Howard
THE DEAD SEA SCROLLS Timothy Lim
DEMOCRACY Bernard Crick
DERRIDA Simon Glendinning
DESCARTES Tom Sorell
DESERTS Nick Middleton
DESIGN John Heskett
DEVELOPMENTAL BIOLOGY Lewis Wolpert
THE DEVIL Darren Oldridge
DIASPORA Kevin Kenny
DICTIONARIES Lynda Mugglestone
DINOSAURS David Norman
DIPLOMACY Joseph M. Siracusa
DOCUMENTARY FILM Patricia Aufderheide
DREAMING J. Allan Hobson
DRUGS Leslie Iversen
DRUIDS Barry Cunliffe
EARLY MUSIC Thomas Forrest Kelly
THE EARTH Martin Redfern
EARTH SYSTEM SCIENCE Tim Lenton
ECONOMICS Partha Dasgupta

EDUCATION Gary Thomas
EGYPTIAN MYTH Geraldine Pinch
EIGHTEENTH-CENTURY BRITAIN Paul Langford
THE ELEMENTS Philip Ball
EMOTION Dylan Evans
EMPIRE Stephen Howe
ENGELS Terrell Carver
ENGINEERING David Blockley
ENGLISH LITERATURE Jonathan Bate
ENLIGHTENMENT John Robertson
ENTREPRENEURSHIP Paul Westhead and Mike Wright
ENVIRONMENTAL ECONOMICS Stephen Smith
ENVIRONMENTAL POLITICS Andrew Dobson
EPICUREANISM Catherine Wilson
EPIDEMIOLOGY Rodolfo Saracci
ETHICS Simon Blackburn
ETHNOMUSICOLOGY Timothy Rice
THE ETRUSCANS Christopher Smith
THE EUROPEAN UNION John Pinder and Simon Usherwood
EVOLUTION Brian and Deborah Charlesworth
EXISTENTIALISM Thomas Flynn
EXPLORATION Stewart A. Weaver
THE EYE Michael Land
FAMILY LAW Jonathan Herring
FASCISM Kevin Passmore
FASHION Rebecca Arnold
FEMINISM Margaret Walters
FILM Michael Wood
FILM MUSIC Kathryn Kalinak
THE FIRST WORLD WAR Michael Howard
FOLK MUSIC Mark Slobin
FOOD John Krebs
FORENSIC PSYCHOLOGY David Canter
FORENSIC SCIENCE Jim Fraser
FORESTS Jaboury Ghazoul
FOSSILS Keith Thomson
FOUCAULT Gary Gutting
THE FOUNDING FATHERS R. B. Bernstein
FRACTALS Kenneth Falconer
FREE SPEECH Nigel Warburton
FREE WILL Thomas Pink
FRENCH LITERATURE John D. Lyons
THE FRENCH REVOLUTION William Doyle
FREUD Anthony Storr
FUNDAMENTALISM Malise Ruthven
FUNGI Nicholas P. Money
GALAXIES John Gribbin
GALILEO Stillman Drake
GAME THEORY Ken Binmore
GANDHI Bhikhu Parekh
GENES Jonathan Slack
GENIUS Andrew Robinson
GEOGRAPHY John Matthews and David Herbert
GEOPOLITICS Klaus Dodds
GERMAN LITERATURE Nicholas Boyle
GERMAN PHILOSOPHY Andrew Bowie
GLOBAL CATASTROPHES Bill McGuire
GLOBAL ECONOMIC HISTORY Robert C. Allen
GLOBALIZATION Manfred Steger
GOD John Bowker
GOETHE Ritchie Robertson
THE GOTHIC Nick Groom
GOVERNANCE Mark Bevir
THE GREAT DEPRESSION AND THE NEW DEAL Eric Rauchway
HABERMAS James Gordon Finlayson
HAPPINESS Daniel M. Haybron
HEGEL Peter Singer
HEIDEGGER Michael Inwood
HERMENEUTICS Jens Zimmermann
HERODOTUS Jennifer T. Roberts
HIEROGLYPHS Penelope Wilson
HINDUISM Kim Knott
HISTORY John H. Arnold
THE HISTORY OF ASTRONOMY Michael Hoskin
THE HISTORY OF CHEMISTRY William H. Brock
THE HISTORY OF LIFE Michael Benton
THE HISTORY OF MATHEMATICS Jacqueline Stedall
THE HISTORY OF MEDICINE William Bynum
THE HISTORY OF TIME Leofranc Holford-Strevens
HIV/AIDS Alan Whiteside
HOBBES Richard Tuck
HOLLYWOOD Peter Decherney
HORMONES Martin Luck
HUMAN ANATOMY Leslie Klenerman
HUMAN EVOLUTION Bernard Wood
HUMAN RIGHTS Andrew Clapham
HUMANISM Stephen Law

HUME A. J. Ayer
HUMOUR Noël Carroll
THE ICE AGE Jamie Woodward
IDEOLOGY Michael Freeden
INDIAN PHILOSOPHY Sue Hamilton
INFECTIOUS DISEASE Marta L. Wayne and Benjamin M. Bolker
INFORMATION Luciano Floridi
INNOVATION Mark Dodgson and David Gann
INTELLIGENCE Ian J. Deary
INTERNATIONAL MIGRATION Khalid Koser
INTERNATIONAL RELATIONS Paul Wilkinson
INTERNATIONAL SECURITY Christopher S. Browning
IRAN Ali M. Ansari
ISLAM Malise Ruthven
ISLAMIC HISTORY Adam Silverstein
ITALIAN LITERATURE Peter Hainsworth and David Robey
JESUS Richard Bauckham
JOURNALISM Ian Hargreaves
JUDAISM Norman Solomon
JUNG Anthony Stevens
KABBALAH Joseph Dan
KAFKA Ritchie Robertson
KANT Roger Scruton
KEYNES Robert Skidelsky
KIERKEGAARD Patrick Gardiner
KNOWLEDGE Jennifer Nagel
THE KORAN Michael Cook
LANDSCAPE ARCHITECTURE Ian H. Thompson
LANDSCAPES AND GEOMORPHOLOGY Andrew Goudie and Heather Viles
LANGUAGES Stephen R. Anderson
LATE ANTIQUITY Gillian Clark
LAW Raymond Wacks
THE LAWS OF THERMODYNAMICS Peter Atkins
LEADERSHIP Keith Grint
LIBERALISM Michael Freeden
LIGHT Ian Walmsley
LINCOLN Allen C. Guelzo
LINGUISTICS Peter Matthews
LITERARY THEORY Jonathan Culler
LOCKE John Dunn
LOGIC Graham Priest
LOVE Ronald de Sousa
MACHIAVELLI Quentin Skinner
MADNESS Andrew Scull
MAGIC Owen Davies
MAGNA CARTA Nicholas Vincent
MAGNETISM Stephen Blundell
MALTHUS Donald Winch
MANAGEMENT John Hendry
MAO Delia Davin
MARINE BIOLOGY Philip V. Mladenov
THE MARQUIS DE SADE John Phillips
MARTIN LUTHER Scott H. Hendrix
MARTYRDOM Jolyon Mitchell
MARX Peter Singer
MATERIALS Christopher Hall
MATHEMATICS Timothy Gowers
THE MEANING OF LIFE Terry Eagleton
MEDICAL ETHICS Tony Hope
MEDICAL LAW Charles Foster
MEDIEVAL BRITAIN John Gillingham and Ralph A. Griffiths
MEDIEVAL LITERATURE Elaine Treharne
MEDIEVAL PHILOSOPHY John Marenbon
MEMORY Jonathan K. Foster
METAPHYSICS Stephen Mumford
THE MEXICAN REVOLUTION Alan Knight
MICHAEL FARADAY Frank A. J. L. James
MICROBIOLOGY Nicholas P. Money
MICROECONOMICS Avinash Dixit
MICROSCOPY Terence Allen
THE MIDDLE AGES Miri Rubin
MINERALS David Vaughan
MODERN ART David Cottington
MODERN CHINA Rana Mitter
MODERN DRAMA Kirsten E. Shepherd-Barr
MODERN FRANCE Vanessa R. Schwartz
MODERN IRELAND Senia Pašeta
MODERN JAPAN Christopher Goto-Jones
MODERN LATIN AMERICAN LITERATURE Roberto González Echevarría
MODERN WAR Richard English
MODERNISM Christopher Butler
MOLECULES Philip Ball
THE MONGOLS Morris Rossabi
MOONS David A. Rothery
MORMONISM Richard Lyman Bushman
MOUNTAINS Martin F. Price

MUHAMMAD Jonathan A. C. Brown
MULTICULTURALISM Ali Rattansi
MUSIC Nicholas Cook
MYTH Robert A. Segal
THE NAPOLEONIC WARS Mike Rapport
NATIONALISM Steven Grosby
NELSON MANDELA Elleke Boehmer
NEOLIBERALISM Manfred Steger and Ravi Roy
NETWORKS Guido Caldarelli and Michele Catanzaro
THE NEW TESTAMENT Luke Timothy Johnson
THE NEW TESTAMENT AS LITERATURE Kyle Keefer
NEWTON Robert Iliffe
NIETZSCHE Michael Tanner
NINETEENTH-CENTURY BRITAIN Christopher Harvie and H. C. G. Matthew
THE NORMAN CONQUEST George Garnett
NORTH AMERICAN INDIANS Theda Perdue and Michael D. Green
NORTHERN IRELAND Marc Mulholland
NOTHING Frank Close
NUCLEAR PHYSICS Frank Close
NUCLEAR POWER Maxwell Irvine
NUCLEAR WEAPONS Joseph M. Siracusa
NUMBERS Peter M. Higgins
NUTRITION David A. Bender
OBJECTIVITY Stephen Gaukroger
THE OLD TESTAMENT Michael D. Coogan
THE ORCHESTRA D. Kern Holoman
ORGANIZATIONS Mary Jo Hatch
PAGANISM Owen Davies
THE PALESTINIAN-ISRAELI CONFLICT Martin Bunton
PARTICLE PHYSICS Frank Close
PAUL E. P. Sanders
PEACE Oliver P. Richmond
PENTECOSTALISM William K. Kay
THE PERIODIC TABLE Eric R. Scerri
PHILOSOPHY Edward Craig
PHILOSOPHY IN THE ISLAMIC WORLD Peter Adamson
PHILOSOPHY OF LAW Raymond Wacks
PHILOSOPHY OF SCIENCE Samir Okasha
PHOTOGRAPHY Steve Edwards
PHYSICAL CHEMISTRY Peter Atkins
PILGRIMAGE Ian Reader
PLAGUE Paul Slack
PLANETS David A. Rothery
PLANTS Timothy Walker
PLATE TECTONICS Peter Molnar
PLATO Julia Annas
POLITICAL PHILOSOPHY David Miller
POLITICS Kenneth Minogue
POSTCOLONIALISM Robert Young
POSTMODERNISM Christopher Butler
POSTSTRUCTURALISM Catherine Belsey
PREHISTORY Chris Gosden
PRESOCRATIC PHILOSOPHY Catherine Osborne
PRIVACY Raymond Wacks
PROBABILITY John Haigh
PROGRESSIVISM Walter Nugent
PROTESTANTISM Mark A. Noll
PSYCHIATRY Tom Burns
PSYCHOANALYSIS Daniel Pick
PSYCHOLOGY Gillian Butler and Freda McManus
PSYCHOTHERAPY Tom Burns and Eva Burns-Lundgren
PURITANISM Francis J. Bremer
THE QUAKERS Pink Dandelion
QUANTUM THEORY John Polkinghorne
RACISM Ali Rattansi
RADIOACTIVITY Claudio Tuniz
RASTAFARI Ennis B. Edmonds
THE REAGAN REVOLUTION Gil Troy
REALITY Jan Westerhoff
THE REFORMATION Peter Marshall
RELATIVITY Russell Stannard
RELIGION IN AMERICA Timothy Beal
THE RENAISSANCE Jerry Brotton
RENAISSANCE ART Geraldine A. Johnson
REVOLUTIONS Jack A. Goldstone
RHETORIC Richard Toye
RISK Baruch Fischhoff and John Kadvany
RITUAL Barry Stephenson
RIVERS Nick Middleton
ROBOTICS Alan Winfield
ROMAN BRITAIN Peter Salway
THE ROMAN EMPIRE Christopher Kelly
THE ROMAN REPUBLIC David M. Gwynn
ROMANTICISM Michael Ferber
ROUSSEAU Robert Wokler
RUSSELL A. C. Grayling
RUSSIAN HISTORY Geoffrey Hosking
RUSSIAN LITERATURE Catriona Kelly

THE RUSSIAN REVOLUTION
S. A. Smith
SCHIZOPHRENIA Chris Frith and
Eve Johnstone
SCHOPENHAUER Christopher Janaway
SCIENCE AND RELIGION Thomas Dixon
SCIENCE FICTION David Seed
THE SCIENTIFIC REVOLUTION
Lawrence M. Principe
SCOTLAND Rab Houston
SEXUALITY Véronique Mottier
SIKHISM Eleanor Nesbitt
THE SILK ROAD James A. Millward
SLANG Jonathon Green
SLEEP Steven W. Lockley and
Russell G. Foster
SOCIAL AND CULTURAL
ANTHROPOLOGY
John Monaghan and Peter Just
SOCIAL PSYCHOLOGY Richard J. Crisp
SOCIAL WORK Sally Holland and
Jonathan Scourfield
SOCIALISM Michael Newman
SOCIOLINGUISTICS John Edwards
SOCIOLOGY Steve Bruce
SOCRATES C. C. W. Taylor
SOUND Mike Goldsmith
THE SOVIET UNION Stephen Lovell
THE SPANISH CIVIL WAR Helen Graham
SPANISH LITERATURE Jo Labanyi
SPINOZA Roger Scruton
SPIRITUALITY Philip Sheldrake
SPORT Mike Cronin
STARS Andrew King
STATISTICS David J. Hand
STEM CELLS Jonathan Slack
STRUCTURAL ENGINEERING
David Blockley
STUART BRITAIN John Morrill
SUPERCONDUCTIVITY Stephen Blundell
SYMMETRY Ian Stewart
TAXATION Stephen Smith
TEETH Peter S. Ungar
TERRORISM Charles Townshend
THEATRE Marvin Carlson
THEOLOGY David F. Ford
THOMAS AQUINAS Fergus Kerr
THOUGHT Tim Bayne
TIBETAN BUDDHISM
Matthew T. Kapstein
TOCQUEVILLE Harvey C. Mansfield
TRAGEDY Adrian Poole
THE TROJAN WAR Eric H. Cline
TRUST Katherine Hawley
THE TUDORS John Guy
TWENTIETH-CENTURY BRITAIN
Kenneth O. Morgan
THE UNITED NATIONS
Jussi M. Hanhimäki
THE U.S. CONGRESS Donald A. Ritchie
THE U.S. SUPREME COURT
Linda Greenhouse
UTOPIANISM Lyman Tower Sargent
THE VIKINGS Julian Richards
VIRUSES Dorothy H. Crawford
WATER John Finney
WILLIAM SHAKESPEARE Stanley Wells
WITCHCRAFT Malcolm Gaskill
WITTGENSTEIN A. C. Grayling
WORK Stephen Fineman
WORLD MUSIC Philip Bohlman
THE WORLD TRADE ORGANIZATION
Amrita Narlikar
WORLD WAR II Gerhard L. Weinberg
WRITING AND SCRIPT
Andrew Robinson

Available soon:

THE WELFARE STATE David Garland
CRYSTALLOGRAPHY A. M. Glazer
SHAKESPEARE'S COMEDIES Bart van Es
COMPUTER SCIENCE
Subrata Dasgupta
ASTROPHYSICS James Binney

For more information visit our website

www.oup.com/vsi/

Kim Knott

HINDUISM

A Very Short Introduction

SECOND EDITION

OXFORD
UNIVERSITY PRESS

OXFORD
UNIVERSITY PRESS

Great Clarendon Street, Oxford, OX2 6DP,
United Kingdom

Oxford University Press is a department of the University of Oxford.
It furthers the University's objective of excellence in research, scholarship,
and education by publishing worldwide. Oxford is a registered trade mark of
Oxford University Press in the UK and in certain other countries

© Kim Knott 1998, 2016

The moral rights of the author have been asserted

First edition published 1998
Second edition published 2016

All rights reserved. No part of this publication may be reproduced, stored in
a retrieval system, or transmitted, in any form or by any means, without the
prior permission in writing of Oxford University Press, or as expressly permitted
by law, by licence or under terms agreed with the appropriate reprographics
rights organization. Enquiries concerning reproduction outside the scope of the
above should be sent to the Rights Department, Oxford University Press, at the
address above

You must not circulate this work in any other form
and you must impose this same condition on any acquirer

Published in the United States of America by Oxford University Press
198 Madison Avenue, New York, NY 10016, United States of America

British Library Cataloguing in Publication Data
Data available

Library of Congress Control Number: 2015952194

ISBN 978-0-19-874554-9

Printed and bound by
CPI Group (UK) Ltd, Croydon, CR0 4YY

Links to third party websites are provided by Oxford in good faith and
for information only. Oxford disclaims any responsibility for the materials
contained in any third party website referenced in this work.

Contents

Preface xiii

Acknowledgements xvii

List of illustrations xix

List of maps xxi

List of tables xxiii

1 The scholar and the devotee 1

2 Revelation and the transmission of knowledge 10

3 Understanding the self 23

4 Divine heroes: the epic tradition 38

5 The divine presence 48

6 Hinduism, colonialism, and modernity 62

7 Challenges to Hinduism: women and *dalits* 74

8 Crossing the black waters: Hinduism beyond India 88

9 Hindu *dharma*, Hinduism, and hinduisms 102

Appendix: The six philosophical systems (*darshana*) 111

Timeline 113

Glossary 117

References 121

Further reading 125

Publisher's acknowledgements 131

Index 133

Preface

Hindu gods and goddesses are everywhere in India, hidden within gorgeous temples and small wayside shrines, depicted in intricate stone carvings, looking out benevolently from advertisements, calendar prints, and film posters, and captured on market stalls and in shop windows in jewellery and small sculptures. They are woven into the fabric of life in Indian villages and cities, and are now also to be found in Hindu communities from the Caribbean to North America and Europe, from South Africa to Thailand. They are much loved by all. The many places in which they appear and the multitude of forms they take indicate the diversity and richness of Hindu culture.

But Hinduism extends beyond culture into other spheres—into the social structure and social life of Hindus, ethical issues, and the politics of equality and nationalism. Contemporary Hinduism and its traditional stories, teachings, and rituals affect so many aspects of the lives of Indians in and beyond the subcontinent that we begin to wonder how to define it. Is it appropriate to call it 'a religion'? Is it like Christianity or Islam? In what ways does it differ? Does it, in fact, challenge our notions of what a religion is?

This introduction to Hinduism begins by raising the question of how different starting points influence the way Hinduism is perceived and understood: how far do the motives and conclusions of Hindu devotees and scholars of Hinduism differ? In the following chapters, the importance to Hindus of early traditions contained in the scriptures, and their subsequent transmission from generation to generation by priests, gurus, and storytellers is considered. An important question discussed and handed down by Hindus over many centuries has been 'Who am I?' or, to put it another way, 'What is the self?' Philosophers have discussed the nature of the self, its relationship to God and the world, whether it continues after death, and how it is affected by human actions. These are still valid issues, as shown in Chapter 3.

Hindu gods and goddesses, including Rama, Sita, Durga, Ganesha, Vishnu, Shiva, and Krishna, the stories told about them, their representation in sculpture and pictures, and their worship are all examined in Chapters 4 and 5. How do Hindus understand the divine in its many forms? Do they worship many gods at the same time, or are these all manifestations of a single divine being? Is there is some truth in both these ideas?

In the 17th and 18th centuries, when Europeans first came into contact with Hindu ideas about the divine, and with Hindu rituals and social life, they were puzzled and shocked. They saw it all through the lens of their own religion and culture, and compared it with their own experience, often drawing unfavourable conclusions. Chapter 6 opens with the relationship of European and American outsiders to Hinduism, and then considers the impact of British colonialism on religious developments in India in recent centuries. Chapter 7 turns to the views of Hindu women and untouchables, *dalits* as they are now known, and considers their changing place within Hinduism.

Challenging questions about who is or is not a Hindu are also raised by Indians who have crossed 'the black waters' and moved beyond the sacred territory of India. Yet, in Indian communities worldwide, temples have been established, Hindu movements have spread, and Hindu ideas and rituals have been transmitted. The spiritual side of Hinduism has appealed to non-Hindus too, raising the question of whether Hinduism remains a religion solely for those born into Indian families and Hindu castes, or whether it is now a missionary religion.

These and other questions about the identity of Hinduism are discussed in Chapter 9. Is it one religion or many different religions each defined by region, caste, and sect? Is it a religion at all? Does it challenge the very idea of religion? Whilst it is impossible to answer these questions fully, opening them up for discussion reveals the extraordinary complexity, diversity, and dynamism of all that we call 'Hinduism'.

Acknowledgements

I am indebted to all those who taught me about Hinduism: my teachers, Hindu friends, and colleagues. Extensive footnotes are not appropriate in an introductory book, and in their absence I express my gratitude to the many whose work helped me to describe and explain Hinduism. Thanks also go to my students of many years on whom I tried out my ideas, and from whom I learnt how to convey such a diverse and challenging subject. Thanks also to those who assisted with the production and publication of the manuscript (and with updating it for this second edition), especially the publisher's readers and reviewers, including the late Julia Leslie. My thanks also to colleagues at the University of Leeds for their support at a time when writing an introductory book was low on the academic agenda.

I benefited immensely from the kindness, imagination, and attention to detail of family and friends who read draft chapters: special thanks to my mother, Kay Knott, my husband, John Murdoch, Ursula King, Eleanor Nesbitt, Ram Krishan Prashar, and Bob Jackson. I had helpful conversations with others in the book's formative stages and in the lead up to the second edition, including Nilaben and Asha Pancholi, Sewa Singh Kalsi, Gavin Flood, Jackie Hurst, Subash Sharma, Bob Exon, Preeti Tyagi, Daphne Green, Jasjit Singh, Arya Burt, Johanna Ahonen, Brian Black, and Anderson Jeremiah.

Writing this book was a pleasure. I have always admired those who could make difficult subjects interesting and approachable without diluting their complexity or distorting their meaning. I thank those at OUP for giving me the opportunity to attempt this for Hinduism. Whether I have done it justice will be best judged by those who give time to reading what follows.

Finally, love and thanks to my daughter, Anita, and—for the second edition, my grandson, Gray—who provided me with joyful and welcome breaks after each day's work. Without 'the spaces in-between', this would have been a lesser book.

List of illustrations

1 Guru and disciples: Nilima Devi and her pupils, Leicester, UK **20**
Reproduced courtesy of the *Leicester Mercury*

2 *Samsara* and *karma*: a diorama of the transmigration of the self **33**
Artwork Courtesy of The Bhaktivendanta Book Trust International, Inc. www.Krishna.com. Used with Permission

3 Dance performance of the *Ramayana*, Kalakshetra School of the Arts, Chennai **39**
© Christopher Pillitz/In Pictures/Corbis

4 A devotee offers milk to Ganesha, 1995 **49**
© Independent, London/Nicholas Turpin

5 A wayside shrine to Shiva and Devi **52**
Reproduced courtesy of Kim Knott

6 Worshipping at a home shrine, Mumbai **56**
Reproduced courtesy of Robert Jackson

7 An etching of *sati* from *India's Cries to British Humanity* by James Peggs, 1832 **72**
Public Domain

8 A woman worshipping at a Shiva *linga*, from the Manley *Ragamala*, *c.*1610 **77**
Reproduced courtesy of the Trustees of the British Museum

9 *Sati* handprints: a memorial to women immolated on their husbands' funeral pyres **86**
Reproduced courtesy of Julia Leslie

10 Greetings from the Shri Swaminarayan Hindu Mandir, London **96**
BAPS Swaminarayan Sanstha

11 A Mumbai street scene **102**
Reproduced courtesy of Kim Knott

List of maps

1 The Indian subcontinent, with religious sites **xxiv**

2 Hindu migrations from India **89**

List of tables

1 The principal Hindu scriptures **13**

2 Varna-ashrama-dharma **18**

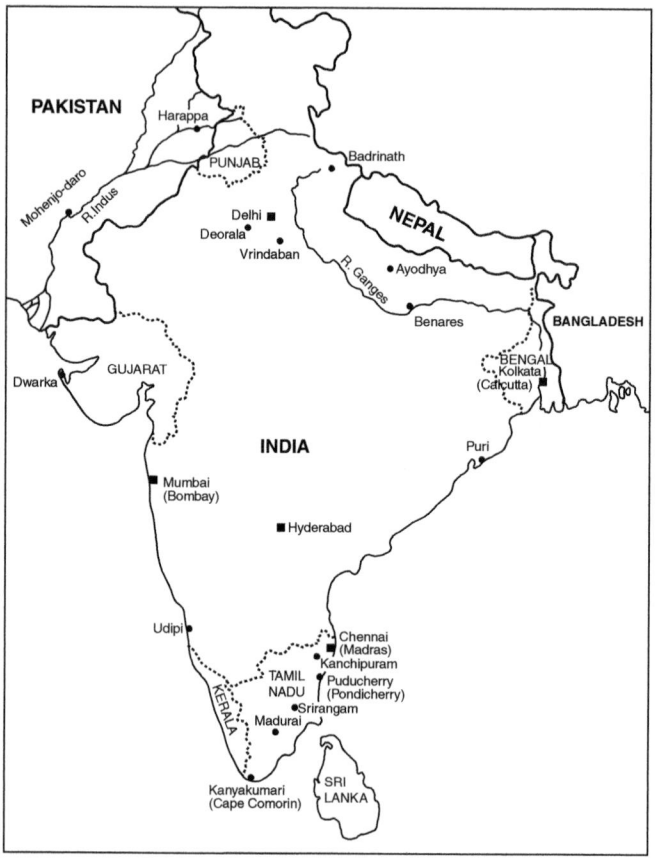

Map 1. The Indian subcontinent, with religious sites.

Chapter 1
The scholar and the devotee

If you go into a library or bookstore with the intention of finding out about Hinduism, to which section do you go? To 'Sociology' for books on the social system of the Hindus? To 'Art and Architecture' to learn about the fabulous temples, carvings, and paintings in which Hindu mythology is depicted? To 'Languages' for books on Sanskrit and other Indian languages? To 'Anthropology' for information about village India, its society and culture? Although you would find useful sources in all these locations, you would probably go first to the 'Religion' section, because in western countries Hinduism is thought of as a religious system much like Judaism, Christianity, Islam, and Buddhism.

One of the key issues for this short introduction is the extent to which this is true. Is Hinduism a religion like others, and what are its principal characteristics? In this book, as well as discussing a particular theme, I ask what that theme reveals about the nature of Hinduism. In Chapter 9 I return to the definition of Hinduism, particularly to the question of unity and diversity. The term 'Hinduism' implies a unified religious system, and indeed many Hindus and non-Hindus describe it in this way. Others, however, say there are many Hindu traditions, even many 'hinduisms': they are related to one another, but remain different in important ways. Is it possible to say which view is right, and to give a watertight definition of Hinduism? Until the final chapter I will follow conventional usage and refer to 'Hinduism'.

Seeing Hinduism from different perspectives

Do people who practise Hinduism see it the same way as those who study it? Do practitioners and devotees share the same perspective as scholars?

Why is this important? In order to choose between the various accounts of Hinduism on offer, it is helpful to understand how those written by scholars and practitioners may differ. The two groups have different intentions and readerships in mind. The former seek primarily to inform; the latter, to encourage spiritual progress. This book is a scholarly rather than a devotional account. Its aim is not to recommend Hindu practices or ideas, nor is it to put forward a particular Hindu viewpoint, but rather to introduce interested readers—Hindu and non-Hindu—to some of the principal characteristics of Hinduism.

Furthermore, even among scholarly books there are those by both *insiders* and *outsiders*, Hindu and non-Hindu scholars. In the West, for example, introductions to Hinduism have been written by those who have studied and written about their own religion, such as K. M. Sen, Anantanand Rambachan, and Arvind Sharma. Others are by scholars who have spent many years studying Hinduism but are not Hindus themselves, like Klaus Klostermaier, Wendy Doniger, and Tracy Pintchman. To what extent does a person's religious persuasion affect what he or she writes about religion? Each book on Hinduism differs as a result of the background and viewpoint of its author. What scholars choose to include or exclude in their books, what examples they give, and how they organize their material are all subjective decisions.

So how does this account differ from other introductory books on Hinduism? As this is '*a very short introduction*', a great deal has had to be left out. I have chosen to write more about contemporary forms and expressions than the history of the religion and its early beliefs and practices. As a woman scholar, I have ensured that Hindu women and those from other poorly represented groups are given sufficient attention. As a white British person, I am historically related to the colonizers of India. I can't change my heritage, but I have tried to think critically about the impact of the British on modern Hinduism. As an outsider—someone who is not a Hindu—I offer a different perspective. I can't draw upon an internal Hindu source of knowledge, so I depend instead upon listening to many Hindu views and opinions for my understanding of the religion in all its complexity.

All writers have their own viewpoint. Readers do too. I hope there will be something for every type of reader in this book, even if it is only something to argue with.

The search for origins

To understand more about differing views of scholars and Hindu practitioners as well as the historical development of Hinduism, I turn to the case of early Indian history. (See also the timeline at the end of the book.)

How do Hindus understand their origins and the early formation of their religion? Many describe Hinduism as *sanatana dharma*, the eternal tradition or religion. This refers to the idea that its origins lie beyond human history, and its truths have been divinely revealed (*shruti*) and passed down through the ages to the present day in the most ancient of scriptures, the *Veda*. Many share this faith perspective, but varying opinions arise when it comes to interpreting human history in early India.

One popular view today, among Hindu nationalists for example, is that divine truth was revealed to the Aryans, whom they see as a noble, enlightened race which lived in India thousands of years ago. As they see it, the Aryans shared a great language, Sanskrit, in which the Vedic scriptures were composed. They built a majestic Hindu civilization, the rituals, literature, and law of which remain the common culture of Hindus today and India's rightful national heritage. According to this view, people belonging to the religions which developed in India after the time of the Aryans, to Buddhism, Jainism, and Sikhism, are all embraced within Hindu culture.

But many other Indians—Hindus as well as Buddhists, Jains, Sikhs, and Christians—do not share this understanding. They challenge the idea that the roots of Hinduism were entirely Aryan. They believe instead that some of the great deities and important religious developments that are now associated with Hinduism came from indigenous, non-Aryan peoples who lived elsewhere in India. According to some, the Aryans were not natives but incomers, migrating into north-west India, conquering peaceful, settled communities, imposing their ideology yet absorbing what was valuable and popular from the surrounding culture. This view has also been widely held by western scholars, who dated the Aryan migration to around 1500 BCE and the *Rig Veda*, the earliest known scripture of the Aryans, to the centuries that followed.

In addition to those who hold one of these two broad views, there are other Hindus whose reconstruction of early Indian history derives from the particular teachings of the Hindu group or sect to which they belong. In short, there is no single agreed account, rather a variety of competing devotional and scholarly perspectives. Furthermore, the material evidence, from archaeological remains, and early epigraphs and texts, does not provide a clear picture, with many questions remaining unanswered for practitioners and scholars alike.

From the mid-19th century onwards, British and Indian archaeologists uncovered the remains of several early cities in the Indus valley region of the Indian subcontinent, dated to 2600–1800 BCE. The society and culture attributed to these cities is commonly referred to as the Indus valley civilization (denoting its location) or the Harappan civilization (Harappa being one of two major cities, Mohenjo-daro being the other). The archaeological evidence suggests that the religion of these cities involved temple rites, fertility rituals, the use of animals, perhaps for sacrifice, and ritual bathing in a large pool constructed of stone. Tiles or seals have been found depicting an early undeciphered script and religious symbols that raise various questions.

Is the seated, horned figure surrounded by animals found on one seal an early depiction of the god Shiva? Are the many female figurines found in the cities and neighbouring villages merely fertility symbols, or are they evidence of a form of goddess worship which has continued unabated throughout the centuries and is still found today? Is the Indus script an early relative of Sanskrit and thus an Indo-European language, or is it a Dravidian language spoken and written by early indigenous people? Was the urban civilization of the Indus valley surpassed by the pastoral society and culture of Aryan migrants, or were all or some of the inhabitants of the cities of Harappa and Mohenjo-daro themselves Aryan?

Indian and western Indologists are actively researching these and other questions in the hope of shedding more light on the early history of India. Another group of Indian scholars uses astronomical data and calculations to date events mentioned in early texts. But how interested people—both scholars and practitioners—then interpret new information and ideas is not a simple matter. They often have theories into which they fit the data. Scholars claim to be guided solely by the available evidence in drawing their conclusions, but we need only to look back to early scholarly work by westerners in India to see how the ideological interests of the time may have affected their work.

Most of the 18th- and early 19th-century scholars (we often refer to them as 'orientalists') who undertook the early translation of Sanskrit texts and the reconstruction of the Aryan past were first and foremost British administrators. In this capacity, they needed to acquire a good understanding of Hindu culture and traditions to support the establishment of British colonial rule in India. Inspired by what they learnt about the similarities between Sanskrit and European languages, and about the Aryan people described in the Sanskrit texts, some drew conclusions about the common origins of Indo-European societies and cultures. The romantic view which they put forward had appeal in Europe and India because it suggested a common descent from noble (*arya*) origins. With its roots in early western scholarship, it was this view, of a great Aryan race and civilization, that later became popular with Hindu nationalists. The leaders of the late 19th-century Hindu movement called the Arya Samaj were among the first to look back to such a golden age and to claim a continuous, unified history for selected Hindu beliefs, values, and practices from that time. What had originally been a colonial scholarly perspective was taken up by this and other groups whose religious and political views it served.

There is a desire among both Indians and those who study India to understand her past and to resolve these difficult issues. But it is not only a matter of uncovering more information in order to complete the jigsaw. Ideological understandings of early history follow their own rules, not those of historical evidence and argument. They may be guided by theological conceptions of divine revelation, or by political interests. Where historical evidence can support such a view, it may be welcomed, but a firm religious conviction does not require such evidence in order to thrive. It depends rather on faith. For members of some Hindu groups, all this argument about what happened in early India is only relevant if and when it accords with the teachings to which they subscribe. There are others, however, who feel strongly that scholarly theories and historical data need not be a threat to faith but can offer important ideas and evidence for an informed perspective.

What happened in the early history of India is just one controversial area which highlights such differences of opinion. The dating and meaning of scripture, and the significance of practical Hinduism are two others.

Understanding scripture and debating Hindu practices

For devout Hindus the *Veda* is revealed; it does not originate at a particular time in history but is eternal and of divine origin. Hindu philosophers such as Shankara and Ramanuja, whose ideas are discussed in Chapter 3, accepted this belief and took it as a cornerstone for their ideas about the relationship between the divine and human. Western specialists of religious texts, however, have been guided by quite different impulses. Those who have studied the *Bhagavad-gita*, the best known of all Hindu scriptures, have been motivated by the principle of scientific rigour in their attempt to date the text, to translate it accurately, and, as they see it, to let it speak for itself rather than reflect the concerns of later interpreters. Some have then gone on to challenge the accuracy of Hindu devotional translations and interpretations. Recently, however, Hindu critics have questioned this approach for its failure to give credence to the role of revelation in Hindu belief and the tradition of devotional commentary. Some of these critics think the western scholarly style of critical reasoning itself distorts the meaning of scripture. They say that revealed texts are only fully understood by those who accept their place within a dynamic, living tradition where verses and stories are heard, repeated, remembered, and passed down. In Chapter 2, Hindu scriptures and their significance are discussed in more detail.

Those orientalists who first studied the religion of the Hindus in the 18th and 19th centuries were strongly influenced by preconceived notions about religion. Their own experience was of western Christianity, a religion characterized by belief in God and his son Jesus, and in God's word revealed in the Bible. They expected the Hindu religion to be similar. So it is perhaps not surprising that they focused upon religious texts such as the *Rig Veda* and *Bhagavad-gita*, and the teachings and laws they contained. They were less interested in the rituals and worldly activities of the Hindus. Where they mentioned them, they often interpreted them critically, seeing them as later additions to what was originally a noble belief system. These scholars intellectualized Hinduism, describing Hindu practices as superstitious and idolatrous, and believing that Hinduism would be a better religion if they were removed, and if theistic, philosophical, and spiritual elements were stressed. Some 19th-century Hindu leaders were themselves influenced by such orientalist views. Ram Mohan Roy, sometimes referred to as the father of modern Hinduism, was opposed to 'idol-worship', 'polytheism', and 'widow-burning' (*sati*). He wrote in favour of monotheism, belief in one God rather than many, and used selected Hindu scriptures and Christian Unitarianism to support his case. He founded a society, the Brahmo Samaj, which was committed to the reform of Hindu practices and the propagation of ideas which bridged Christian and Hindu thought. A few western-educated Hindus accepted these ideas, but the majority did not. Orthodox brahmins defended their traditions. They were joined by a western scholar, H. H. Wilson, who argued that rituals like *sati* were part of Hindu tradition and should not be meddled with by interfering, though well-meaning, outsiders. (For more on 19th-century figures and movements, see Chapter 6; for meanings of Sanskrit terms, see the Glossary at the end of the book.)

One writer, Nirad Chaudhuri, who wrote with energy about these debates in the late 1970s, concluded that Hinduism should not be defined so much by its spiritual and philosophical traditions as by its *worldliness*, its focus on things like the acquisition of wealth and love and the practice of duty. He argued that the ritual, devotional, and social practices of the followers of Krishna, Shiva, and the Goddess had too often been ignored in western accounts. An important aspect of Hinduism, he believed, is power. Hindus are concerned with seeking divine assistance in order to acquire and use this power for desired ends and rewards.

Scholars and practitioners have been motivated by different principles in their ideas about Hinduism, its history, scriptures, and practices. But there have also been differing opinions within each camp. Some non-Hindu scholars have tried imaginatively to enter Hindu world-views, whereas others have viewed them through the lens of their own colonial or Christian interests. Some Hindus have developed a sense of critical distance towards their religion, while others have been nurtured according to tradition and guided principally by faith. In Chapter 2, I look more closely at the way Hindus learn about their traditions, and the value they place upon retaining them and passing them down to the next generation.

Chapter 2
Revelation and the transmission of knowledge

Storytellers and *Shankara-acharyas*: handing down Hindu teachings

Sitting bolt upright, cross-legged on the cool clay-washed floor of his house, he may be seen any afternoon poring over a ponderous volume in the Sanskrit language mounted on a wooden reading stand, or tilting towards the sunlight at the doorway some old palm-leaf manuscript. When people want a story, at the end of their day's labours in the fields, they silently assemble in front of his home, especially on evenings when the moon shines through the coconut palms…he is completely self-reliant, knowing as he does by heart all the 24,000 stanzas of the *Ramayana*, the 100,000 stanzas of the *Mahabharata*, and the 18,000 stanzas of the *Bhagavata*. If he keeps a copy of the Sanskrit text open before him, it is more to demonstrate to his public that his narration is backed with authority.

The Pandit (as he is called) is a very ancient man, continuing in his habits and deportment the traditions of a thousand years…He has unquestioned faith in the validity of the *Vedas*, which he commenced learning when he was seven years old. It took him twelve years to master the intonation of the *Vedas*…Even the legends and myths, as contained in the puranas, of which there are eighteen major ones, are mere illustrations of the moral and spiritual truths enunciated in

> the *Vedas*. 'No one can understand the significance of any story in our mythology unless he is deeply versed in the *Vedas*,' the storyteller often declares. Everything is interrelated.

R. K. Narayan's storyteller in *Gods, Demons and Others* (1964) embodies an important Hindu notion, that traditional stories and the truths they contain are worthy of repeated retelling. He is a medium or channel, one who by his public recitation brings Hindu teachings to a ready audience. His duty is great and his task important: to recite the age-old stories from the scriptures, to thrill his audience with tales of Rama and Sita, Radha and Krishna, to show their contemporary relevance, and to continue the chain of storytelling from his father and grandfather. His work embodies the notion of tradition and its continuity through the generations. Like some other Hindu specialists, he imparts what he himself once learnt.

The Sanskrit word for this is *sampradana*, meaning 'giving' or 'teaching'. A related term is *sampradaya*, oral tradition, which is generally used to indicate an institution centred round a guru in which theological and ritual traditions are passed down and sustained from generation to generation. There are many *sampradayas* in contemporary Hinduism, some of which are discussed in Chapter 3, which are linked to early teachers by means of a lineage or chain of disciples. One example is the *sampradaya* which follows from the 9th-century teacher, Shankara, and continues today in monastic institutions in different parts of India. These are places of learning where monks train in Sanskrit and philosophy, and where ordinary Hindus come to worship and seek guidance from a guru. They are headed by renowned leaders known as *Shankara-acharyas (acharya* means 'leader' or 'master'). Before taking on the mantle of religious authority, these leaders receive a traditional training undertaken by many brahmin boys in which they learn to recite the *Veda*. As youths they are also instructed by their gurus in the teachings of the *sampradaya*. Once selected as future leaders, they travel for many years as gurus in their own right, giving spiritual advice and helping people to carry out their religious duties. They are then initiated into the role and responsibilities of *Shankara-acharya*. They are known for their personal charisma, wisdom, and piety, but also as bearers of the great tradition of Shankara, assisting the passage of his teachings through the generations.

The *Shankara-acharyas* are brahmins; they are also gurus. In both capacities they fulfil the important function of handing down knowledge. Although the two roles are brought together in the *Shankara-acharya*, this is not always the case. Gurus may come from any caste group, and brahmins need not be spiritual guides, though many are. What brahmins and gurus transmit and how they do so may be quite different, as this chapter will show.

Shruti and *smriti*: revelation and tradition

In Chapter 1, I referred to the importance of that which is 'revealed', *shruti*. This term refers to the manifestation of the divine in the world, particularly to the truths revealed to the early sages or *rishis* which were later brought together in the form of scriptures. There are different views among Hindus about which scriptures are *shruti* and which fall into the other important category of sacred literature, *smriti*, that which is 'remembered' or 'handed down'. *Smriti* texts are based upon revealed truth, but are of human composition. A common division between the early texts is set out in Table 1.

The *Vedas* and *Upanishads* constitute the *shruti* literature and are said to have been divinely revealed; the Epics, *Puranas*, and *Sutras* are said to have been taught by sages and remembered by their disciples (*smriti*). The *Veda* contains accounts of creation, information about ritual sacrifice, and prayers to the gods. The *Rig Veda*, the earliest of the Vedic texts, is a collection of hymns to the gods. Agni, the deity associated with fire and sacrifice, was one

Table 1. The principal Hindu scriptures

Shruti	Smriti
Veda: There are four collections which constitute the *Veda*. They are known as *Rig Veda*, *Sama Veda*, *Yajur Veda*, and *Atharva Veda*. The first three contain hymns and mantras; the fourth, spells and charms. These are the earliest known Hindu scriptures. There are three other types of *shruti* literature: the *Brahmanas*, the *Aranyakas*, and, of most importance, the *Upanishads*. ***Upanishads***: The word *upanishad* means 'sitting near' and implies that these texts were secret scriptures taught by a sage to a disciple. The principal *Upanishads* include *Brihadaranyaka*, *Chandogya*, *Katha*, *Maitri*, and *Shvetashvatara*. *Shruti* scriptures are commonly dated by scholars between 1500 and 300 BCE. They were all composed in Sanskrit.	**Epics**: The earliest scriptures identified as *smriti* are the *Mahabharata*—which includes the *Bhagavad-gita*—and the *Ramayana*, dated between 500 BCE and 100 CE. These are long poems which narrate episodes in the lives of great warriors. Krishna appears in the first; Rama has a central role in the second. ***Sutras***: In the same period, a number of texts about important subjects such as *dharma*, *yoga*, and *vedanta* were composed (see the glossary). They contained statements or aphorisms (*sutra* means 'thread'). An important text from this period was the *Manusmriti*, which dealt with Hindu law and conduct. ***Puranas***: Mythological texts known as *Puranas* followed in the period from 300 to 900 CE. They refer to earlier events, often telling the stories of the gods and goddesses. Principal texts include *Markandeya Purana*, *Vishnu Purana*, *Vayu Purana*, *Shiva Purana*, and *Bhagavata Purana*.

of the most popular. He was petitioned because, as fire, he was accessible to people and could bring light. He was addressed as a messenger who could communicate between humanity and the other gods.

> I pray to Agni, the household priest who is the god of the sacrifice, the one who chants and invokes and brings most treasure. Agni

earned the prayers of the ancient sages, and of those of the present too; he will bring the gods here. Through Agni one may win wealth, and growth from day to day, glorious and most abounding in heroic sons. Agni, the sacrificial ritual that you encompass on all sides—only that one goes to the gods. Agni, the priest with the sharp sight of a poet, the true and most brilliant, the god will come with the gods. Whatever good you wish to do for the one who worships you, Agni, through you, O Angiras, that comes true. To you Agni, who shine upon darkness, we come day after day, bringing our thoughts and homage to you, the king over sacrifices, the shining guardian of the Order, growing in your own house. Be easy for us to reach, like a father to his son. Abide with us, Agni, for our happiness. *Rig Veda* 1.1

Most Hindus accept the status and authority of the *Veda*. Very few will have read it, although they will have heard parts of it chanted in Sanskrit during important ceremonies. The more popular texts, which are often known intimately by Hindus, are the *Mahabharata* and the *Ramayana* (see Chapter 4). The former includes the 'Song of the Lord' or *Bhagavad-gita*, in which Krishna teaches the warrior Arjuna about the importance of doing one's duty, as well as how to achieve liberation from suffering and repeated rebirth. So beloved are these texts that they are sometimes referred to as a fifth *Veda*, and considered by many to be divinely revealed.

Other types of literature are important, too, and are given varying status by different groups of Hindus. The *Tantras*, texts from the 8th and 9th centuries acclaimed in Kashmir, Bengal, and Nepal, focus on spiritual discipline, ritual activity, and the attainment of magical powers. They often take the form of a dialogue between Shiva and the Goddess. They are significant for Tantric Hinduism, which has special doctrines and rituals that differ from those of the brahmins. Also popular is devotional or *bhakti* poetry, composed in local Indian languages. One notable example is the collection of Tamil songs to the god Vishnu by the 10th-century poet Nammalvar from south India. Such is its stature, it is often referred to as the 'Tamil *Veda*'.

According to R. K. Narayan's storyteller, all India's myths and stories derive their significance and authority from the *Veda*. Many Hindus would agree with him, seeing later Tantric and devotional texts as the culmination of the *Veda*; others would see them rather as a challenge to Vedic religion. However, so great is the importance of the *Veda* in the authorization of many later scriptures and in brahminical orthodoxy that some commentators have seen it as the defining aspect of Hinduism. In an important text on Hindu law from the 2nd century BCE, called *Manusmriti*, the author, Manu, declared that the *Veda* should not be questioned and that those who did so were beyond the pale. An American scholar, Brian K. Smith, has suggested that Hindus are those people who use the *Veda* as a reference point for the creation, maintenance, and transformation of their traditions. By this definition, Buddhists, Jains, and Sikhs, who deny Vedic authority and the role of brahmins in conveying and interpreting it, are clearly not within the Hindu fold.

The brahmin and the transmission of ritual knowledge

Although the concepts of *shruti* and *smriti* refer to sacred literature, they are also important for understanding the figures mentioned earlier in this chapter and their religious roles. Brahmins, gurus, and storytellers, in their different ways, are all channels for the truth once revealed, then remembered and orally transmitted through history. The hymns of the *Veda*, which were heard and recited by the early sages, became the responsibility of brahmin families who passed them on from father to son, unchanged down the centuries (to recipients like Narayan's storyteller).

The language of Sanskrit offers a range of related terms—*brahman*, brahmin, *Brahmanas*, and Brahma—leading to potential confusion about their application and meaning. Here is a guide to their meaning:

brahman: This originally referred to creative power or truth, inherent in Vedic hymns and later in the sacrifice during which they were recited. By the time of the early *Upanishads*, it had come to refer to the impersonal cosmic principle or absolute reality.

brahmin: A ritual specialist associated with *brahman*; one who recites Vedic hymns and performs the sacrifice; priestly caste. Also known as *brahmana* and *brahman*.

Brahmanas: Texts having to do with *brahman* in which Vedic sacrifice is described.

Brahma: The Hindu god associated with creation.

In a famous verse from *Rig Veda* 10.90, the class of people known as brahmins were identified with the mouth of the cosmic person, Purusha; his arms, thighs, and feet becoming the other classes of society (*varna*). The brahmins were thus linked in Vedic society with language and communication, with the recitation of Vedic hymns and formulas (*mantra*), and, ultimately, with the sacred power inherent within them.

When British administrators first conversed with brahmins in India in the 18th century they were astonished to find that Vedic scriptures had been passed down accurately in oral form—not learnt from written texts—by the ancient process of transmission in which brahmin boys in the student stage of life learnt by imitation of their elders. Even today, some young brahmins learn to recite Vedic mantras in the traditional way, though modern printing, secular education, and the Internet have led to the scriptures being read by many people in new ways.

However, these brahmin males not only recite Vedic mantras for their own sake, to keep divine revelation alive, but they also carry out

rites to sustain the world and to maintain the relationship between humanity and the gods. They are associated with *dharma*, which is sometimes translated as religion, but more properly as truth, law, duty, or obligation. *Dharma* has both a general and a personal application. The harmony of the world must be maintained, and an individual's *dharma* must be fulfilled. The work of the brahmin supports both of these requirements. By performing sacrificial rituals (*yajna*) similar to those mentioned in the *Veda*, brahmins make offerings to the gods in the sacred fire and petition them to sustain the natural world and benefit their patrons. Then, in special rites associated with the life cycle (*samskara*), they initiate Hindus into new roles. By giving the sacred thread in the *upanayana* ceremony, they convey the status of 'twice-born' upon young males. In marriage they bind together husband and wife and set them off on the householder stage of life. In rites surrounding childbirth, brahmins ensure the correct entry into society of the new-born baby and help to rid the family of the pollution arising from the birth. And, finally, in the ceremonies associated with death, they facilitate the smooth transition of the soul and make sure the ancestors are correctly served.

Brahmins are not involved in the disposal of the body of the deceased as this is considered too polluting a task for one whose power derives in part from his ritual purity. Similarly, there are other rituals outside their sphere of activity, such as the propitiation or exorcism of dangerous spirits. Ritual specialists from other caste groups for whom purity is not so important are responsible for these. They too may have inherited the necessary practical knowledge and mantras from their caste elders. The concept of *varna-ashrama-dharma* conveys the idea of duties or obligations which fall to a person according to their particular social class and stage of life (see Table 2). Men who were not 'twice-born' and had no access to Vedic teaching were not expected to follow the same stages of life as those in the higher groups. Married women's obligations were generally referred to as *stri-dharma*, the duties of the wife.

Table 2. Varna-ashrama-dharma

Varna, social class	*Ashrama*, stages of life
The four traditional Aryan social classes (*varna*) were identified in *Rig Veda* 10.90 with parts of the body of the cosmic Purusha: mouth—brahmins (*brahmana*) arms—warriors (*kshatriya*) thighs—commoners (*vaishya*) feet—servants (*shudra*) The *varnas* were organized hierarchically. The first three classes were called 'twice-born', with boys being given a sacred thread in an initiation ceremony (*upanayana*). Only 'twice-born' males were entitled to hear the *Veda*. The *shudra* class may have been added to the others in order to accommodate the local non-Aryan population.	Four stages of life were described in later Hindu texts, though originally they were seen not as stages but as alternative life-choices. Only 'twice-born' males undertook the four *ashramas*, which were the stages of: student (*brahmacharya*) householder (*grihastha*) forest dweller (*vanaprastha*) renouncer (*sannyasa*) Following their early years in their father's home, young women were married. Marriage was seen as their rite of initiation into the duties of a wife.

Strictly speaking, class (*varna*) and caste (*Jati*) are different social institutions, though castes are often assumed to fit into the four *varnas*. *Jati*, which means 'birth', is a system of social divisions organized according to relative purity, with brahmins at one end of the spectrum, and low caste and 'untouchable' or *dalit* people, who are considered impure and polluting to so-called 'higher' castes, at the other. Although the caste system is not based on wealth but on ritual purity and pollution, it is certainly the case that those at the 'lower' end have less access to resources such as land and economic power.

Indians acquire caste status by being born into a particular caste group; they generally marry someone from the same caste. In earlier times, castes were also occupational groups, though urbanization and industrialization have meant that many people are now working in quite different jobs to those with which they were traditionally associated. Because of the link between purity, pollution, and caste, a person's caste can also influence their social relationships, particularly with whom they may eat and where they live. Untouchables or *dalits* are often forced to live outside the village, away from those of higher castes. The Constitution of India outlawed untouchability and it was made a punishable offence in the 1950s, but change has been very slow and the situation of India's untouchables continues to be a social ill in need of urgent treatment (see also Chapter 7).

The guru and the transmission of spiritual knowledge

The author R. K. Narayan was very interested in religious figures, their social position, charisma, and authority. In *The Guide* (1958) he wrote about an ex-prisoner who, taking shelter in a temple one day after his release from jail, is mistakenly thought to be a holy man. He finds himself giving advice and telling homiletic stories (remembered from his mother's knee), then fasting to bring an end to the drought which endangers the livelihood of the villagers. He is held in awe, assumed to be above temptation and weakness, to be able to intercede with God, and to have spiritual gifts arising from his ascetic practices. He is thought to be wise and to know what is best for people. These are some of the characteristics often associated with a guru, one who can enlighten others and can help them cross the ocean of repeated death and rebirth (*samsara*) to gain liberation (*moksha*).

Who is fitted for this task? Does it require the Sanskrit training of the brahmin or the storyteller's knowledge of mythology?

As Narayan's guide shows, the key to a guru's authority lies in charisma rather than in caste tradition, formal training, or even virtue. Some gurus have no secular or Vedic education. Some are illiterate. But they all have the knowledge acquired through their own spiritual experience plus a profound ability to use this to good effect in helping others (see Figure 1).

Anandamayi Ma was one such guru. She was born in a village in what is now Bangladesh in 1896 and, despite marrying and becoming a housewife, she became a spiritual practitioner and guide to many. She was different in many ways to the *Shankara-acharyas* described earlier because she was not part of a traditional institution. She was not formally initiated, nor was she trained in her youth for religious responsibilities. While she was from a brahmin household, as a woman, she had not been given a Vedic education, but had been married when she was 13 years old.

1. Guru and disciples: Nilima Devi and her pupils, Leicester, UK.

For several years after settling with her husband's family she regularly chanted the names of God and sat in meditation, often becoming fully absorbed and unaware of what went on around her. Then, when she was 26, she had an extraordinary experience of inner initiation (*diksha*) in which she believed she was given her own mantra, a word or verse on which she could meditate. In a deep sense, as she reported later, she came to realize that the guru, the disciple, and the mantra were all one. They were not separate.

This realization bears a strong resemblance to that described by some other Hindu mystics. It is identified by philosophers in the tradition of Shankara as an experience of *brahman*, the one absolute reality that is both the universal principle and the self or spiritual aspect of each person (see Chapter 3). However, Anandamayi Ma was not concerned with philosophical speculation or debate, but rather with witnessing to the truth and helping those who sought her out. Like many other gurus, she travelled extensively, meeting disciples of all castes and sharing her observations. She spoke practically, alluding to the natural world, relationships, and everyday life. Her advice to people on how to make spiritual progress was simple and undemanding: she invited them to find a regular time to commit themselves to the truth, a time when they would endeavour to be moderate in their habits, would serve others as manifestations of the divine, and would strive for tranquility. She encouraged them to do as she had done, to chant or meditate, and gradually to realize their own true nature.

She passed on the knowledge she had acquired through her own experience in much the same way as Hindu mothers do when they tenderly nurture their children in the rituals and stories handed down within their own families. She was referred to by many, including those of other religions, as 'Ma' or mother. But, like other gurus, she was also childlike, revelling in her experience of the divine, and joyfully sharing it with others.

Anandamayi Ma represents the continuity of a tradition from the time of the *Upanishads* in which a disciple seeks wholeheartedly for spiritual truth and is guided by the inner self to enlightenment. She is said to have attained what is known as *jivanmukti*, liberation within this life. She became someone who was sought out by others for the wisdom she could impart. How Hindus understand this inner self and the truth it reveals is discussed in Chapter 3.

Chapter 3
Understanding the self

Twenty-first century gurus have continued to teach and guide their disciples by traditional methods while also employing up-to-date communications technology. A number of gurus maintain an international following in this way. Successful guru-based groups such as the Swaminarayan Hindu Mission, the Sri Mata Amritanandamayi movement, the International Society for Krishna Consciousness (ISKCON), and the Shaiva Siddhanta Church have centres in and beyond India, with their leaders travelling around the globe to visit disciples. The last of these was led, until his death in 2001, by a guru called Sivaya Subramuniyaswami, an American by birth and *Shaiva* Hindu by initiation. He used the medium of the magazine *Hinduism Today* (available in print and online) to reach out to new and established disciples and other interested people. From the 'Publisher's Desk' in November 1994, Sivaya Subramuniyaswami gave his answer to the question 'Who Am I?'

> Rishis proclaim that we are not our body, mind or emotions. We are divine souls on a wondrous journey. We came from God, live in God and are evolving into oneness with God. We are, in truth, the Truth we seek. Aum.
>
> We are immortal souls living and growing in the great school of earthly experience in which we have lived many lives. Vedic rishis have given us courage by uttering the simple truth, 'God is the Life

> of our life.' A great sage carried it further by saying, there is one thing God cannot do: God cannot separate Himself from us. This is because God is our life. God is the life in the birds. God is the life in the fish. God is the life in the animals.
>
> Becoming aware of this Life energy in all that lives is becoming aware of God's loving presence within us. We are the undying consciousness and energy flowing through all things.

Committed Shaiva Siddhanta disciples and enquirers may follow up their questions about life energy, God, and the soul online by joining a Facebook group, subscribing to the Church's YouTube channel, or via email or Twitter. This is a new version of the old idea found in the *Upanishads*, of a seeker enquiring of a sage about the truth. Preliminary answers to existential and practical questions can be obtained online irrespective of distance and regardless of caste, nationality, gender, or religion. Deep and effective spiritual transmission, however, requires *darshana*, seeing and being seen by the guru. An innovative approach is offered by Amma (Shri Mata Amritanandamayi Devi) who purifies, heals, and teaches her followers by hugging them. Seeing the world and its people as an extension of herself, her embraces are an expression of unconditional love.

To explore further Hindu ideas about the self, it is instructive to go back to a much earlier story in which a disciple enquires of his guru. Picture a young man called Shvetaketu, and his teacher, who is none other than his father, Uddalaka Aruni. Shvetaketu has already studied the *Vedas* and, thinking himself learned, has returned to his father's home. There, his father discovers that, despite years of study, his son has not fully comprehended the true nature of reality. Using the analogy of the fig, Uddalaka demonstrates how the same essence is in everything: the quality of the fig is in the fruit, the seeds within it, and the tree which grows from it. To press his point further, the father then instructs his son using the example of salt:

'Put this chunk of salt in a container of water and come back tomorrow.'

The son did as he was told, and his father said to him: 'The chunk of salt you put in the water last evening – bring it here.' He groped for it but could not find it, as it had dissolved completely.

'Now, take a sip from this corner,' said the father. 'How does it taste?'

'Salty.'

'Take a sip from the centre.— How does it taste?'

'Salty.'

'Take a sip from that corner.—How does it taste?'

'Salty.'

'Throw it out, and come back later.' He did as he was told and found that the salt was always there. The father told him: 'You, of course, did not see it there, son; yet it was always right there. The finest essence here—that constitutes the self of this whole world; that is the truth; that is the self (*atman*). And that's how you are, Shvetaketu!'

(*Upanishads*: *Chandogya Upanishad*, 6.13)

'That's how you are' is a translation of a famous Sanskrit phrase, 'Tat tvam asi'. It expresses the idea that the truth which underlies everything and is its essence is also identical with Shvetaketu's own self (*atman*). This truth or self is the life force (*brahman*) within both the world and humanity. These three important words, 'Tat tvam asi', are considered to contain a vital truth about the nature of reality, and to have the power to bring about self-realization. As well as appearing in the *Upanishads*, this and other important phrases are found in a later compendium of aphorisms known as the *Brahma-sutra* or *Vedanta-sutra*. This text summarized the teachings of the *Upanishads* on ultimate reality (*brahman*), and became pivotal within a philosophical system known as *vedanta*. *Vedanta* was one of six orthodox systems (*darshana*) within Hinduism; the *yoga* system was another (see Appendix).

To understand more about *vedanta* and what it teaches about the self, I turn to three early philosopher-theologians, and consider how their ideas have continued to be significant for modern Hindu movements. Shankara, Ramanuja, and Madhva were south Indian brahmins acknowledged for their skill in philosophical exposition. Each offered a different interpretation which, while consistent with *vedanta* tradition, was pertinent to the time in which he lived (see Box 1).

When westerners were first introduced to Hindu spirituality at the end of the 19th century by a travelling teacher called Vivekananda (see also Chapter 6), what they encountered was a modern interpretation of Shankara's ideas about *vedanta*. From him they learnt that the impersonal, ultimate reality was also the personal God that people worshipped, and that this God was also the higher self within each human being: 'He is you yourself,' said Vivekananda (echoing 'Tat tvam asi').

This modern version of Shankara's non-dualist *vedanta* became so widespread in the West that many commentators assumed it to be synonymous with Hinduism as a whole.

Box 1 *Vedanta* and Vedantins

Vedanta is a philosophical system in which scholars have focused upon the study of Vedic texts concerning ultimate reality (*brahman*). Of particular importance for study were the *Upanishads*, the *Bhagavad-gita*, and the *Brahma-sutra*. There have been many Vedantins, scholars of *Vedanta*, three of whom have been especially influential in the history of Hindu thought and practice. Their views have ranged from an understanding of the relationship between ultimate reality and the self as identical (Shankara) to an understanding of their separation and difference (Madhva).

Shankara (788–820 CE) Non-dualist or *advaita vedanta*	Ramanuja (1017–1137 CE) Qualified non-dualist or *vishishtadvaita vedanta*	Madhva (13th century CE) Dualist or *dvaita vedanta*
The Order founded by Shankara continues today in Sringeri, Dwarka, Badrinath, Puri, and Kanchi. The impact of Shankara's ideas has also been felt through Vivekananda, the Ramakrishna Order, and the Vedanta Society in the USA. Mata Amritanandamayi, the 'hugging mother', is a contemporary guru in this tradition.	The Shri-Vaishnava Order of which Ramanuja was a leader, and in which his philosophy is taught, continues today with its centre in Srirangam in south India. The Gujarati Swaminarayan Movement is one of several *sampradayas* which claim disciplic succession from Ramanuja.	The temple and monastery at Udipi which were established by Madhva in the 13th century continue today. The International Society for Krishna Consciousness (and the Bengali Gaudiya Vaishnava Math in which it has its origins) claims a disciplic link to Madhva via the 16th-century charismatic figure Chaitanya.

They weren't aware that there were other equally persuasive and quite different perspectives on the divine and its relationship to the human self. When seekers and scholars began to visit India in large numbers in the 1960s and 1970s, they met with gurus and movements representing other approaches to *vedanta*. The widespread popularity of devotional, theistic Hinduism, underpinned by the theological ideas of Ramanuja and Madhva and their later disciples, was apparent throughout India and further afield among migrant Hindus. From the traditional Shri Vaishnava *sampradaya* in south India to the modern movements of the Swaminarayans in Gujarat and the Hare Krishnas (ISKCON) in Bengal and beyond, the devotional theology which had challenged early non-dualist ideas about ultimate reality and the self was flourishing.

But what were these ideas, and why have they been so important for the development of Hinduism?

Shankara

Advaita means 'non-duality'. Used to describe Shankara's perspective on *vedanta*, it indicates the inseparability of the salt and the water in the story about Shvetaketu. To Shankara, in the 9th century CE, ultimate reality and the self were identical, and his task was to explain why people failed to realize this. One of the ways in which he did this was by referring to the example of the traveller who mistook a rope for a snake, superimposing a false impression (a snake) upon the truth (the rope). He listed the many ways in which different people understood—or rather misunderstood—the self, for example, by equating it with the body, the sense organs, or the mind. All these imposed a false idea upon the self (*atman*). To Shankara, *atman* was really none other than *brahman*. There was no plurality of consciousness or being. It was all one. Liberation was achieved by removing ignorance, learning to discriminate between what was eternal and what only masqueraded as such, and then acquiring knowledge of the self's identity with *brahman*.

To the brahminical community, Buddhism remained a significant threat in India, so Shankara cleverly borrowed scholarly methods used earlier in Buddhist philosophy in order to reassert brahminical ideas. By acknowledging a lower, conditioned level of knowledge in which distinctions, like those between the rope and the snake, were recognized, he was able to explain the importance given in the *Veda* to ritual activity and sacrifice to the gods. He distinguished this from the higher or absolute level in which all is one and reality is experienced as non-dual.

Ramanuja

Teaching more than two centuries later in another religious context, Ramanuja's task was different. Unlike Shankara, he did not have to combat the popularity of Buddhism, but was committed instead to promoting the religion of the *Vaishnavas*, the followers of the god Vishnu, by giving philosophical support to their devotional claims. Ramanuja worshipped Vishnu and was well versed in the Epics, *Puranas*, and the poetry of his region. His ideas built on the work of Shankara, which, by Ramanuja's time, was accepted by the brahmin community and considered orthodox. He agreed that ultimate reality was non-dual, but disagreed profoundly with Shankara on the nature of *brahman*, the individual selves, and the world. He was pointed in his criticisms, accusing Shankara's followers of error and a lack of insight, and building his own case with examples from a wide range of scriptures.

His main claim was that the strong conviction we have that we are different from one another and from God is not false, as Shankara claimed it to be. The conclusions of our senses and feelings are not illusory. They indicate a profound truth, that ultimate reality is internally qualified (*vishishta*). What is more, ultimate reality is not impersonal and without qualities, as Shankara asserted. Ramanuja saw it as *ishvara*, the Lord, the one who is desired by all those who seek to escape from suffering. As such, *brahman* is none other than the supreme person or God of the *Mahabharata*, *Ramayana*, and *Puranas*.

But what, then, is the relationship between the self and this supreme person? God is the inner controller of both the individual selves and the world. Ramanuja said that, just as the human body is the instrument of the self within, so the world and the selves are related to God.

Knowledge of God helps to lead people to liberation, but God's grace and the self's surrendering response are vital, too.

Madhva

Madhva had a good deal of sympathy with this view, but his reaction to Shankara's ideas was different again. Renouncing the world and joining a *Vaishnava* Order at 16, he learnt about *vedanta* and gradually developed his own critique (*dvaita*). Like Ramanuja, he utilized a full range of Vedic, Puranic, and later devotional texts, but went further, concluding that the teachings of scripture can only be understood as dualistic, as maintaining a complete distinction between the Lord and the self. *Brahman* and *atman* were not identical. What is more, he saw the selves as different from one another, and from the world. Even within the world, he understood phenomena to be distinct. Everything existed within the will of the supreme Lord while maintaining its own particularity. To be liberated from suffering and rebirth required divine grace, dependence on God, and active devotion, worshipping the Lord in the form of an icon (*murti*). Madhva placed such an icon of Krishna in his monastery in Udipi where it remains to be seen by pilgrims to this day.

Although each of these three philosopher-theologians composed commentaries on the key *vedanta* texts, they drew distinctive conclusions, for example, on the meaning of the phrase we encountered in the story of Shvetaketu: 'Tat tvam asi', 'That you are'. For Shankara, this signified non-duality; there was no difference between that ultimate reality and the self. For Ramanuja, unity was not implied. Instead, the sentence suggested that *brahman* (*tat*) and *atman* (*tvam*) were distinguished from one another though clearly related. For Madhva, the two were wholly separate, though he saw the self as being in God's image and inhabited by a divine inner witness.

Although these three were the most renowned scholars or *vedantins*, there were others, most of whom, like Ramanuja and Madhva, were *Vaishnavas* who extolled the glories of Vishnu or Krishna. Others, particularly those who revered the god Shiva, have worked outside the tradition of *vedanta*, drawing on Tantric texts in order to develop their theological ideas.

Today, these philosophical conclusions continue to be heard and discussed by disciples within the religious institutions associated with Shankara, Ramanuja, and Madhva. The *Shankara-acharyas* discussed in Chapter 2 continue to preach *advaita-vedanta*. The Shri-Vaishnavas of south India are the natural successors of the theology of Ramanuja. The monastery in Udipi still teaches the devotional dualism of Madhva. The Shaiva Siddhanta Church mentioned at the beginning of this chapter perpetuates the theology developed by earlier *Shaiva* theologians. Earlier this century, many commentators saw Shankara's non-dualism as the epitome of Indian intellectual achievement, but, more recently, an awareness of the vitality of Hindu devotional movements has helped to reassert those theistic perspectives which focus on the loving relationship between devotees and their chosen deity.

These philosophical ideas are not really a matter for everyday discussion by the majority of Hindus, but they do underlie the way in which Hindus think about the divine. Whether a Hindu believes in an ultimate impersonal reality or a personal God has important consequences for his or her religious practice and spiritual journey. Acquiring more knowledge of ultimate reality and its relationship to the self is vital for the former; prayer and worship are central to the latter. One religious idea to which all Hindus make frequent reference, however, is *karma*.

Karma, *yoga*, and the self

No discussion of Hindu views of the self would be complete without a consideration of two familiar notions, *karma* and *yoga*. They are household words, not only in India but also in the West, where *karma* is often associated with fatalism and reincarnation, and *yoga*—usually *hatha yoga*—is practised to improve health and well-being. They were mentioned in the *Upanishads* and *Bhagavad-gita*, were discussed by Shankara, Ramanuja, and Madhva, but were also known to the renouncers of early India—including Mahavira and the Buddha—who withdrew from worldly activities.

Those who know the story of the Buddha will be aware that early Indian society in his time was viewed by spiritual seekers as a place of misery and unrest. Happiness was transitory, to be replaced all too soon by ageing, disease, and death. As scholars have shown, it was also a time of social and political change, with towns emerging, and the agrarian lifestyle and its social organization being eroded. With urban development came greater opportunity for mobility and communication. New ideas travelled as well as people. Many of those who had renounced society to wander and practise the ascetic life shared the view that an individual's personality or self transmigrated at death to a new body, and that this cycle of rebirth (*samsara*) was fuelled by a chain of cause and effect linked to action (*karma*) (see Figure 2). All living things were subject to this and, although good actions might bring about felicitous results and a better rebirth, the suffering and inevitability inherent in the process were seen by many as intolerable. Liberation from continual rebirth was sought, with renouncers attempting by various means to break the cycle, by isolating themselves from society, undergoing fasting and mortification, surrounding themselves with the reminders of suffering and death, and withdrawing into themselves in meditation. By such means, action and its results would cease and liberation would be possible.

2. *Samsara* and *karma*: a diorama of the transmigration of the self.

The problems associated with action and rebirth were addressed several centuries later in the *Bhagavad-gita*. Here, we find Arjuna enquiring of his charioteer, Krishna, about whether he should go into battle against his own kin. Krishna, who, despite his disguise, is really the supreme Lord, offers him guidance like a guru, arguing the case for dutiful action, explaining the journey of the self and the paths to its liberation. He explains to the perplexed Arjuna that the embodied self or soul does not die in battle, but passes into a new body: 'It cannot be pierced, it cannot be burned, it cannot be wetted, it cannot be parched. It is invariable, everywhere, fixed, immovable, eternal' (2.24). He reminds Arjuna of his social and religious duty (*dharma*) as a member of the warrior class, and goes on to teach him about the discipline of action (*karma yoga*).

Arjuna assumes that Krishna's view, like that of the ascetics, is that action is to be renounced. Krishna's response comes loud and clear: 'A man does not attain freedom from the results of action by abstaining from actions, and he does not approach perfection simply by renunciation' (3.4). He goes on to explain that it is the results of action which are to be renounced, not action itself—one should not desire particular rewards, nor think proudly of oneself as the doer of great deeds. One should be satisfied in the self, offering action and its fruits as a sacrifice to the Lord. This is the discipline of *karma yoga*. Having taught this, Krishna goes on to explain other worthy paths which, pursued steadfastly, will bring a seeker to equanimity and, finally, liberation. *Jnana yoga*, the path of knowledge, and *bhakti yoga*, the way of devotion (see Chapter 5) are given particular attention by Krishna, who reveals himself later in the *Bhagavad-gita* as the universal Lord in whom all seekers may find shelter.

In the sixth chapter of the *Bhagavad-gita*, Krishna discusses the practice of the *yogin*, though he recommends this path only to those capable of great self-control and determination. He describes how such a person should be seated, should control his senses and urges, and should focus his mind. Concentration on the self, quelling the passions, and becoming calm are the hallmarks of this path, the goal of which is bliss. What Krishna describes here is not the more physically strenuous *hatha yoga*, in which practitioners hold difficult postures; nor is it the *siddha yoga* of adepts who have acquired the powers of levitation and telepathy, and the ability to disappear or to withstand pain. It is akin to the practice referred to by Patanjali in his *Yoga-sutra* as *raja yoga*, the royal or highest *yoga*, a meditative *yoga* in which the pinnacle of achievement is *samadhi*, deep concentration leading to liberation of the self.

In the *Bhagavad-gita* Krishna puts forward two innovative ideas: first, *karma yoga*, offering ordinary seekers the possibility of giving spiritual meaning to their everyday actions; and, second, the notion that there is not one way but many ways to liberation, with seekers finding the path most suited to their temperaments and stations. Krishna did not forget those who were traditionally marginalized by brahminical religion. Women and the low born were also recognized as seekers and invited to offer themselves, their actions, and the simple gifts of water, a flower, a leaf, or fruit to Krishna.

The *Bhagavad-gita* transforms the earlier pessimistic notion—that the results of action lead to continual rebirth and transmigration of the self—into a positive discipline for personal transformation. In more recent times, *karma* and *karma yoga* have again been endorsed. Religious nationalists like Bal Gangadhar Tilak and Mahatma Gandhi recommended *karma yoga* in India's struggle for self-rule and as a path of self-realization for busy, modern Hindus. A contemporary Hindu scholar, Arvind Sharma, has also considered their importance for rethinking the issue of caste.

In *Rig Veda* 10.90 and Chapter 2 of the *Bhagavad-gita* we were introduced to the idea of the four classes of brahminical society. Arjuna, as a warrior, was expected to do his class duty and not be tempted to mimic the duties of others just because they seemed more palatable or worthy, or less contentious. This idea of social duty was discussed in greater detail in the *Manusmriti*, where the consequences of neglecting one's duty were treated very seriously. Undutiful or *a-dharmic* actions would be punished with expulsion from one's social group or with a lower rebirth in the next life.

Arvind Sharma tackles this problem head on in *Hinduism for Our Times* (1996). He believes that the link between *karma* and the caste-based society of India needs to be understood and transformed. As he says, 'In the standard Hindu view one's birth in a particular caste is determined by one's *karma* in a previous life.' Hindus take on a caste identity at birth, being born into a family within a particular *jati*, as the argument goes, because of actions in a previous life. The self, in absolute terms, is untainted by this, but, as each self is embodied, it finds itself within a particular caste with all the associated duties and conditions.

It is easy to be fatalistic about this state of affairs, and many Hindu teachers, following Krishna's example in the *Bhagavad-gita*, have offered spiritual advice for tackling it. Arvind Sharma's contemporary solution goes as follows. To think fatalistically about *karma* is unhelpful when, in fact, as human beings we have the power at any moment to change our own behaviour, and thus its consequences for our future. Free will rather than fatalism characterizes the operation of *karma*. What is more, if we accept that *karma* is not so much a process of cause and effect *between* lives as *within* a single life, this changes things. What we do at this moment has consequences for what will happen to us in a few minutes, next week or in ten years' time. One modern life of seventy or eighty years' duration is equal to what might have been three separate lives in the past when life was short and hard (with one birth into a single caste group, where three might previously have been the norm). What becomes important in this view is not caste as an index of past-life *karma*, but present *karma* and its consequences for a person's evolving self-realization and relationships with others. Refocusing *karma* in this way, according to Sharma, undermines the importance of caste and its iniquities. A society in which everyone recognizes that they have an immediate responsibility for improving tomorrow's world rather than their next life will be one in which caste status as a measure of previous actions will disappear. It is the teachings of Krishna on the importance of acting in the world while renouncing the results of one's actions, he says, which make this possible.

Chapter 4
Divine heroes: the epic tradition

What were 80 million Indians doing at 9.30 every Sunday morning in 1987?

They were sitting down in homes and tea-shops—anywhere there was a television—to watch the unfolding drama of the god Rama, his wife Sita, and his brother Lakshmana in the television epic, the *Ramayan*. No one was bored, even though they knew the story already. In fact, when it concluded initially, after 52 weeks, some viewers went so far as to go on strike to demand that further episodes be produced to complete the story (and another 26 were then made). On another occasion, shortly before the denouement, when the villain Ravana was to be killed, fans made long journeys to the television studio to plead for his life. This was no ordinary soap opera. Described by its now famous director, Ramanand Sagar, as a divine phenomenon, it inspired widespread devotion, even a temporary sense of national unity, with Sikhs and Muslims as well as Hindus in its cast and among its viewers. It was more akin to ritual performance than film narrative, with the actors, costumes, lines, sets, and special effects chosen and designed to create a sense of a divine world rather than a human one. The actors became identified with the gods and demons they portrayed, with people touching their feet and seeking their blessings.

3. Dance performance of the *Ramayana*, Kalakshetra School of the Arts, Chennai.

This popular Indian story of Rama, told, remembered, and retold over two and a half millennia, is known to all Hindus and to a great many other people around the world. Hindu infants hear it from parents or other relatives. School children learn about it at the time of the festival of *Divali*. Villagers hear it from storytellers or see it enacted in folk theatre (*ramlila*) and puppet shows (see Figure 3); and now those with computers, laptops, tablets, and mobile phones, as well as televisions and video players, may play and replay their favourite sequences on YouTube.

Although onlookers marvelled at the phenomenal success of the TV *Ramayan*, even praised it for its ability to deliver a religious subject and ethical issues to so large an audience via a commercial medium, nevertheless, it was not without its detractors. Criticisms were directed at its sentimentality, sexism, lack of subtlety, and overstated morality. Some despised the mood of national submissiveness it seemed to engender. Perhaps the most telling criticism for those interested in its religious significance was that it gave authority to a particular version of the story and its associated values and ideas.

The *Ramayana* or story of Rama exists in possibly thousands of versions. The most widely known is the one attributed to Valmiki and passed down to him by the sage Narada, but there are many other written versions and innumerable oral ones. They focus on different characters, many on Rama himself, others on Sita, and some on the demon Ravana, showing him not as evil but as strong and brave, although perhaps misguided, even as an anti-hero or committed rebel. There are *Ramayanas* in scores of languages, and there are traditions of their rendition and performance in the countries of south-east Asia, Africa, Europe, and North America as well as the Indian subcontinent.

Do the many different versions and genres through which the story of Rama is communicated point to a more profound diversity—of Hindu traditions, communities, and practices, indeed of 'hinduisms', related loosely to one another by a narrative thread? This is is discussed further in Chapter 9.

Ramayana, the story (according to Valmiki)

Dasharatha, the king of Ayodhya, by means of sacrifice, is blessed with several sons born to his three wives. Rama, the eldest and much beloved by Ayodhya's citizens, is to succeed him as king. However, Rama's stepmother, Kaikeyi, fearing for herself and her own son Bharata, exacts a promise from Dasharatha that Rama be banished to the forest and Bharata installed as ruler. Rama, obedient to his father's reluctant request, agrees to go. Sita, his devoted wife, won by Rama in a conquest of strength, and Lakshmana, his loyal younger brother, demand to be allowed to accompany him. They leave the city, followed soon after by Bharata who pleads with Rama to return. Rama will not break his vow, and Bharata returns to Ayodhya, placing Rama's sandals on the throne and ruling as regent in his absence.

Rama, Sita, and Lakshmana settle in a hermitage after wandering in the beautiful forest and meeting its ascetic inhabitants. They are discovered there by the sister of the demon Ravana, who tries to entice Rama and destroy Sita. Wounded by Lakshmana, she hurries to her powerful brother, ruler of Lanka, and tells him what has occurred. Ravana, stirred by the account of Sita's beauty, determines to capture her. With the help of another demon, who as a deer lures away the two brothers, Ravana kidnaps Sita by disguising himself as a holy man. He takes her to his city in Lanka.

Rama and Lakshmana enlist the help of the monkeys to find and free Sita. Rama first helps the monkey prince, Sugriva, whose situation mirrors his own. Sugriva then sends his monkeys in search of Sita. It is the divine monkey Hanuman who finds her on Lanka and assures her of her forthcoming release. He is captured but escapes, returning to Rama with his intelligence of Sita's whereabouts. Rama and his army of helpers cross to Lanka on a bridge of monkeys, destroy Ravana, and return valiant with Sita. Rama is reluctant to accept Sita because of the time she has spent in Ravana's household. She undergoes an ordeal by fire to persuade him of her virtue.

Rama becomes king on their return to Ayodhya, but rumours continue about Sita's chastity. Unwillingly, Rama banishes her and she takes refuge with Valmiki (by whom this account is told). She gives birth to Rama's twin sons and later leaves the world, disappearing into the earth from which she first arose. The grieving Rama then ascends to heaven with his followers.

Dharma and the *Ramayana*

With the diverse tellings of the Rama story go different interpretations, but a common theme in many is *dharma*. As I noted in Chapter 2, *dharma* is an important concept in Hinduism signifying order, law, duty, and truth. Men were expected to follow their own *dharma* (their *sva-dharma*) according to their social class, *varna*, and stage of life, *ashrama*, hence the term *varna-ashrama-dharma*. The maintenance of social order in the world and the relationship between humanity and the gods were the corporate responsibility of all, though each person's behaviour in the service of *dharma* was different. The principal text in which these duties (and those of women) were codified was the *Manusmriti* (or Laws of Manu), but in Valmiki's *Ramayana* we witness *dharma* played out through the righteous decisions and actions of Rama, his father, wife, brothers, and loyal devotee, Hanuman. Each has his or her own path to follow in service of the right ordering of the society to which they belong.

The *Ramayana*, like that other great epic, the *Mahabharata*, is a story about the warrior community. Brahmins and ascetics play their part, but their roles are secondary to those of Ayodhya's ruling family, and the monkey and demon warriors. It is a study of kingship, but also of human roles and relationships.

Why does Dasharatha do what Kaikeyi asks of him and banish Rama when it seems to go against the future interests of Ayodhya? And why indeed does Rama agree, in the full knowledge that Ayodhya's citizens want him as their king? Good order is founded on truthfulness and obedience. Dasharatha, as a husband and ruler, must not break his promise, and Rama, as a son, must obediently accept the decisions of his father. He understands his banishment as his destiny and argues against Lakshmana—who is full of indignation—by stressing the binding nature of a father's words. Rama's conduct, seen against his brother's unwillingness to accept the situation, is presented as exemplary.

Sita's behaviour and her relationship with Rama provide further opportunities for the enactment of *dharma*. A wife is not expected to fulfil *varna-ashrama-dharma*; she must fulfil her duty as a daughter, then as a wife (*stri-dharma*). Sita's decision to follow Rama into the forest, despite his protestations, and her chaste commitment to him during her time in Ravana's court are the proper actions of a devoted and dutiful wife (*dharma-patni*).

Why, then, does Rama, having seen the proof of her virtue in the fire ordeal, banish her after their return to Ayodhya? To readers used to romantic endings this might seem heartless. But within a Hindu universe the proper ordering of society rather than the desire of the individual was of first importance. Again, Rama must think and act according to his *dharma* as king. He must give this role priority over and above his personal inclination or belief in Sita's chastity. His own failure to protect his wife from Ravana and *a-dharma* or disorder had led to doubt in the minds of his subjects, and stilling their fears and the social disorder which might follow became his primary duty, despite his knowledge of her innocence. In the Valmiki *Ramayana*, Rama is the ideal—if unhappy—king to the last. Or almost to the last, for towards the end of the story Rama is referred to as an incarnation (*avatara*) of the great god Vishnu. Like Krishna in the *Mahabharata*, Rama, as God in human form, comes into the world to vanquish the forces of *a-dharma* and to exemplify righteous conduct (see Chapter 5).

Sita, Devi, and the goddesses

> *First cousin*: 'Why do we not stage the fight between the good King Ram and the demon King Ravan?'
>
> *Me*: 'Could I play Ram?'
>
> *Second cousin*: 'No, you are a girl.'
>
> *Me*: 'It is only a play.'
>
> *Third cousin*: 'Why do you not play Ram's wife, the good queen, Sita?'
>
> *Me*: 'But Sita does not *do* anything. She is only, well, good.'

In this conversation between the young Madhur Jaffrey—now a world authority on Indian food—and her male cousins, we glimpse one reaction to Sita. 'Dutiful', 'loyal', 'good', and 'beautiful' would be the qualities which might first spring to mind to describe her. But even in Valmiki's story, Sita's strength and self-possession are apparent. She is dutiful, indeed, but she has to argue her case in order to do what she knows to be right. She shows self-control and she doesn't give in to Ravana's will. On being freed, she defends herself wholeheartedly against Rama's accusations. She is far from passive.

This strength of character has not gone unnoticed by Indian women, who have found much in her to applaud. Despite being commonly held up as a paragon of the submissiveness, obedience, and loyalty that many men would like to see in their wives, women have often taken other lessons from her behaviour. 'How was it from your point of view?' asked a British Hindu poet, Debjani Chatterjee, inviting Sita to tell her side of the story. In Sita's fire ordeal Chatterjee sees the all too frequent dowry deaths of contemporary Indian women, and in her banishment she sees the trials of a modern single mother (for dowry deaths, see Chapter 7). Sita's story, she concludes, is no fairy-tale.

In some of the other *Ramayanas* Sita takes on a still different light. In the popular 15th-century Hindi version by Tulsidas she is depicted with heroic strength, being able to lift the great bow of the god Shiva. In the Tamil *Iramavataram* she is shown as justifiably angry and sarcastic, driven to verbal aggression by her harsh, accusing husband. In Nina Paley's 2008 animation, *Sita Sings the Blues*, she exemplifies the plea of women for equal treatment. But it is in women's folk songs that she is most vividly portrayed. The important events of her life as a woman are told—her puberty, wedding, pregnancy, and the birth of her sons—as well as what happens to her in the forest, on the island of Lanka, and during her ordeal. The words of the songs suggest that the women singers understand intimately Sita's experiences and feelings, the way in which she is misunderstood by her husband, and the trials she has to suffer. She is like them.

Sita is a great heroine rather than a goddess. When Hindu women want to pray to a goddess or fast for her blessings, it is not Sita they choose. Parvati, the clever goddess who can intercede with Shiva, or Durga, the powerful warrior, or Kali, the terrifying mother, are called on for help. Superhuman, they are renowned for their divine powers and their capacity to grant the requests of those who worship them. In Hindu mythology they are many, but they are also seen as expressions of the one great Devi, revered by many Hindus as their saviour and guide. Her story is told in the *Devi-Mahatmya* (part of the *Markandeya Purana*). There she is named as one who is prosperous, yet fierce and passionate, a great mother, a refuge, a divine destroyer, a benevolent goddess, a protectress. These qualities are manifest in her particular forms as Lakshmi, Durga, Amba, Kali, Parvati, and many others. But she is also given titles with universal significance. She is called *Mahamaya*, great illusion, and *Shakti*, creative power. She is associated with the supreme gods, Vishnu and Shiva, but is herself seen as the queen or sovereign one. Here is her story.

Devi-mahatmya, the story

Assured that he cannot be killed by any man, Mahisha, the buffalo demon, defeats the world and warns the god Indra that he will soon conquer heaven. They fight and Indra withdraws, seeking the shelter of the great gods, Brahma, Shiva, and Vishnu. They are filled with anger, and from their divine bodies a beautiful woman issues forth: Devi. They provide her with weapons; other gods give her a lion to ride and wine to drink. Her terrifying laugh is heard and the gods shout, 'Victory'.

Hearing this, Mahisha sends his demons to see what is happening. They report to him of her beauty and great qualities, and he sends her a proposal of marriage. She refuses and slays his messengers, and when Mahisha himself follows, she proclaims her mission to protect *dharma*. In the ensuing battle he takes many forms, but she drinks wine and, from the back of her lion, kills him with her trident and discus. The gods are full of praise for Devi's achievement.

Devi breaks the brahminical image of the woman as dutiful wife. She will not marry and cannot be controlled by male demons or gods. She is warlike and aggressive, not submissive and unassertive. She appears to be an ideal woman, being beautiful and amorous, but she drinks wine and is independent. And, in another story, she manifests the still more terrifying Kali from her angry brow, Kali emerging bedecked with severed heads and arms, dripping blood from her lolling tongue. Yet the great power of Devi can be yoked not only by the gods but also by those who praise her devoutly and make offerings to her. To such worshippers (*Shaktas*), though without husband or child, she is the great protective mother.

The Mother, Rama, and the Hindu nation

The images of the protective mother and the dutiful king have inspired loyalty and devotion in India. Both have been used in the modern period as symbols associated with the nation. *Bharata Mata* or Mother India is a familiar concept to Indians of many religions, drawn on in the early 20th century by the Indian National Congress party, which chose as its national anthem the poem *Bande Mataram*, 'Hail Mother'. It is still evoked today with the cry 'Bharata Mata ki jay', 'Long live Mother India'.

Rama is also hailed by Hindu nationalists, as divine ruler of the longed-for Hindu state. It was in Ayodhya in north India in 1992 that extremist Hindus destroyed the Babri mosque because they believed it to be built on the site of a more ancient temple marking the birthplace of Rama. The historical facts are much disputed, but the popular religious imagination thrives not on factual evidence but on powerful stories and the feelings they arouse. Two stories fuelled this imagination in the early 1990s: one, the story of Lord Rama, revisited each week on television, and the other, a contagious rumour about a mosque on ground sacred to the Hindus. Inflamed by the campaigns of pro-Hindu groups and the rhetoric of a Hindu nationalist political party, the mosque was razed to the ground. Communal violence ensued in Indian cities, and both Muslims and Hindus died.

Rama's role as divine ruler of an ideal state continues to be a powerful theme that is often drawn on in India politics. Indeed, Narendra Modi, leader of the Bharatiya Janata Party (BJP), invoked Rama and his rule during the 2014 election campaign which saw him become Prime Minister.

Chapter 5
The divine presence

'Miracle', 'hallucination', 'simple scientific explanation', 'divine grace', or 'politically inspired hoax' ran the headlines as onlookers sought to explain why, on 22 September 1995, images of the god, Ganesha, the world over drank milk offered to them by their devout followers (see Figure 4). The old debate between science and faith was rekindled. Hindus themselves were quietly divided over the phenomenon, but their surprise was not so much at its occurrence as at its scale. Divine manifestations and small miracles are believed to be commonplace in Indian religious life, but what was extraordinary was that Hindus around the globe should witness Ganesha's gracious act.

Ganesha is a much-loved elephant-headed deity revered by Hindus for his kind attention to the requests of his devotees and his ability to remove obstacles. The son of Shiva and Parvati, he was created one day by his mother in order to protect her while she bathed. Shiva, unaware of his son's identity, decapitated him for failing to allow him entry to Parvati's quarters. To appease his distressed wife, Shiva promised to restore his son to life with the head of the first creature to pass by. That creature was an elephant. Like other Hindu deities, Ganesha is depicted with a unique vehicle or mount, his being a rat. A lover of sweets, he is always shown as rotund.

4. A devotee offers milk to Ganesha, 1995.

Statues, idols, or icons?

How can a statue drink? There are scientific and psychological explanations, of course, but how do Hindus explain it? First, it is important to understand the difference between statues and icons (*murtis*). The stone sculptures covering the outside of Hindu temples, the bas reliefs and cave carvings found throughout India all vibrantly depict the iconography of the gods and goddesses and the stories of their feats. They are of great artistic merit and were lovingly carved. But only exceptionally would they be considered worthy of worship. The icon *inside* the temple, however, has been created and installed by a ritual process which has prepared it to be inhabited by God. Religious texts describe the meditative approach of the sculptor, the proportions of the icon (and the temple in which it is to be placed), and the characteristics of the deity who will reside in it. Once formed, brahmins consecrate the image, establishing various deities in different parts of its body and infusing it with living breath (*prana*). From that point on, the divine is manifest within the icon and must be cared for, served like an honoured guest, and offered love. An intimate, reciprocal relationship between devotee and deity is then possible through *darshana* or seeing. Hindus visit their local temples or take trips to more distant pilgrimage sites to take *darshana*, that is, to see and be seen by Krishna, Devi, Shiva, or another deity of their choice.

In the 17th and 18th centuries European traders and travellers first witnessed Hindus taking *darshana*. They wrote critically in their letters and diaries of 'idol-worship', and their responses were reiterated by later Christian missionaries. The traveller, Pierre Martin, in the early 18th century wrote: 'You would scarce believe me, shou'd I name the vile and infamous creatures to which they pay divine honours. 'Tis my opinion that no idolatry among the antients was ever more gross or more horrid, than that of these Indians.' His negativity was reiterated a century later by the Revd Henry Martyn who recorded his observation that, 'In the centre of the building was the idol, a little ugly black image, about two feet high, with a few lights burning round him... I shivered at being in the neighbourhood of hell.' Such worship was considered abhorrent and misguided, particularly by Protestant Christians who believed God was apprehended in the word not the image. They were also aghast at the multiplicity of 'idols', concluding that the Hindus were a polytheistic people, believing in many separate gods and goddesses. From their perspective, though fascinating, this was quite wrong. Their God, though in three persons—father, son, and holy spirit—was but one God.

These commentators did not grasp the theological reasoning behind what they saw—they simply took it at face value. But Ramanuja and the *vedantins* of later centuries, for whom love of Vishnu or Krishna was all-important, taught that the divine manifested in five forms: (i) in the supreme transcendental form; (ii) in its emanations (*avatara*); (iii) in the heart or self of each individual; (iv) as the inner controller of the universe; and (v) as the divine presence within the consecrated icon (*murti*). The divine is transcendent and supreme, but also immanent and accessible. Graciously, as we saw with Rama in the *Ramayana* and Krishna in the *Bhagavad-gita*, the divine may take form as an *avatara* to help humanity in times of need.

The divine is more approachable still as the consecrated temple deity. In the Radha-Raman temple in Vrindaban, in the region of Krishna's childhood where he sported with the cowherd boys and girls and wooed Radha, he allows his devotees to serve him with loving devotion (*bhakti*) and to fulfil all his needs. With Radha, he is offered many different things including water for washing and drinking, clothes, flowers, incense, food, and praise in a ritual called *puja*. They are awoken, dressed, visited by devotees, worshipped, and put to rest each day. Within *Shaiva* and *Shakta* theology and practice, in which Shiva and Devi are respectively the focus, similar ideas and activities may be observed. However, whereas the temple icons of Vishnu, Krishna, and the goddesses have the appearance of humans (in fact, humans are made in *their* image), Shiva rarely manifests as such. He inhabits the *linga*, his sign, a smooth, cylindrical stone (see Figure 5). *Lingas*, like icons of Krishna and Durga, are fashioned and ritually installed in temples, but they also occur naturally. Where they are found in nature they may be worshipped as Shiva despite being unconsecrated.

The many and the one

From the time of the later *Upanishads*, Vishnu and Shiva became popular deities, considered worthy of worship and service by their followers, who were referred to respectively as *Vaishnavas* and *Shaivas*. Cultic practices and doctrinal teachings evolved, and in their stories or myths, recorded in the *Puranas*, they were described iconographically. Shiva was depicted as a Himalayan ascetic, Vishnu as a blue youth holding in his four hands a discus, mace, conch, and lotus. To their followers each was understood to be the supreme, transcendent Lord, but also immanent, dwelling

5. A wayside shrine to Shiva and Devi.

within each person. Shiva was associated with a divine family, through whom his powers were extended. Vishnu asserted his divine influence by taking animal or human form in periods of darkness and moral degradation. By the end of the Puranic period ten principal incarnations or *avataras* had been recorded. These were Matsya, the fish, Kurma, the tortoise, Varaha, the boar, Narashimha, the man-lion, Vamana, the dwarf, Parashurama or 'Rama with the axe', Rama, Krishna, Buddha, and Kalki, 'the white horse' who will come at the end of the dark age or *kali yuga*.

Rama and Krishna have also been seen as independent deities, supreme in their own right. Rama is depicted as a warrior with bow and arrows, escorted by his wife Sita, brother Lakshmana, and devoted servant Hanuman, the monkey warrior. Krishna is most commonly shown as a young flute-playing cowherd boy, surrounded by cows, playing with friends, or teasing the cowherd girls (*gopis*). His favourite is Radha, and in paintings and temple iconography they are often shown together. Krishna is occasionally depicted as a mischievous baby or as the charioteer who accompanies Arjuna, hero of the *Bhagavad-gita*.

Returning to Ganesha, it was not only his temple manifestations which in September 1995 were said to drink the milk offered them by devotees, but also the images in people's homes. Similarly, on other occasions, pictures of gurus and saintly people have been seen miraculously to produce holy water or ash. Divine activities do not seem to be limited only to forms which have undergone ritual consecration. Many Hindu theologians stress both the power and grace of God or the Goddess, and this is mirrored in the non-theological imagination by an understanding that the divine may appear or give a sign at any time, to encourage or reward devotees, to warn them, even to punish them. Stories from the *Puranas*, local traditions, and anecdotal accounts of the experiences of relatives and neighbours repeat and confirm this idea.

A compelling example of this is the way in which female spirits are to be found outside Indian villages, in fields, trees, rocks, and bushes. Signs of the response to their presence are witnessed everywhere: pieces of cloth tied to branches, food and other offerings left by the wayside, stones decorated with silver foil, red paint, or powder. Such signs are evidence of the placation of a female *bhut* or ghost, or a *mata* or local goddess. *Bhuts* are avoided for fear of their displeasure, but *matas* are worshipped to gain favours or blessings. These female spirits linger near the places where, in life, they met untimely and inauspicious deaths or died childless. Some of those women worshipped as *matas* may have ended their lives as *sati* on the funeral pyres of their husbands.

People as well as objects may reveal the presence of the supernatural. We have already seen that the self or *atman* is eternal and divine, whether it is considered to be identical with or separate from ultimate reality or God. Those whose actions show them to be self-realized are often described as *mahatmas* or great selves. Gandhi, who will be discussed in Chapter 6, was one of these. There are others, however, who exhibit the divine in a rather different way—through possession. Once possessed, it is not they who speak or act, but the god or goddess through them. In Kerala, at festival time, the *teyyam* deities possess brilliantly adorned dancers who then walk among the assembled crowds giving *darshana*. And during *Durga Puja* in Bengal and other parts of north India, some devotees are inhabited by the Goddess, who then dances among her followers, answering their questions, and giving them advice. Her presence in such a gathering is considered auspicious, a blessing to all.

If the divine manifests in so many forms and places, were early European visitors correct in assuming Hinduism to be polytheistic? There are certainly a multitude of deities worshipped by Hindus, but, according to the *Upanishads*, the many and the One are not unrelated. A seeker asked the sage Yajnavalkya how many gods there are:

> 'Three and three hundred, and three and three thousand.'
>
> 'Yes, of course,' he said, 'but really, Yajnavalkya, how many gods are there?'
>
> 'Thirty-three.'
>
> 'Yes, of course,' he said, 'but really, Yajnavalkya, how many gods are there?'
>
> 'Six.'
>
> 'Yes, of course,' he said, 'but really, Yajnavalkya, how many gods are there?'
>
> 'Three.'
>
> 'Yes, of course,' he said, 'but really, Yajnavalkya, how many gods are there?'
>
> 'Two.'
>
> 'Yes, of course,' he said, 'but really, Yajnavalkya, how many gods are there?'

'One and a half.'

'Yes, of course,' he said, 'but really, Yajnavalkya, how many gods are there?'

'One.'

Upanishads: Brihadaranyaka Upanishad, 3.9.1.

A great many Hindus favour a particular god or goddess, their *ishtadeva* or chosen one. Family tradition generally determines this, though some people may develop a special relationship with a deity, perhaps one who has answered their prayers at a time of need or who has come to them in a dream. But they also recognize and offer worship to many others. Similarly, in the stories where one god is pre-eminent, tales are told of his relationship to other deities. The divine—which Hindus may perceive as *brahman*, or Devi, or Krishna, or another—manifests in many names and forms, and, in this sense, the many are an expression of the One. Yet both remain important. Hinduism is both polytheistic and monotheistic. Both the many and the One have a place within it, and within the everyday experience of most Hindus.

Responses to the divine presence

How do Hindus respond to the divine in their midst? They make offerings to deities and propitiate spirits, but they respond in other ways, too. Most Hindus have a home shrine in their kitchen (this being the most pure place in the house) or in another room (see Figure 6). There they have images and pictures of their chosen deities and of holy people. To these they may offer food, water, incense, and light each day. While some Hindus also make regular visits to a nearby temple for *darshana*, most attend only at times of festivals (when they may also fast, eat special foods, visit relatives, and give presents).

The festive calendar varies throughout India, depending on local traditions, favoured deities, and the presence of sacred sites. Such places may become centres of attraction to pilgrims at certain

6. Worshipping at a home shrine, Mumbai.

times in the year—perhaps at the anniversary of the resident god or goddess, or in commemoration of a mythic or historical event. Probably the best-known occasion is the *Kumbh Mela (mela* means 'fair') held every three years at pilgrimage centres on the banks of sacred rivers. Thousands of holy people gather there, including the *Shankara-acharyas*, other religious leaders, and their ascetic followers (*sannyasis*). They are joined by millions of Indian pilgrims, many of whom make a once-in-a-lifetime visit to the *mela* to bathe, take *darshana* of the spiritual throng, and receive blessings.

There are many festivals celebrated in India, and they vary from region to region (see Box 2). Even the start of the New Year differs, for some falling in October and for others in April. The calendar which is used to work out festival dates is not like the western Gregorian one. Instead it is lunar, with each of the twelve months having a dark and light half coinciding with the phases of the moon. Different lunar days are considered either auspicious or inauspicious for the worship of particular deities, for activities such as fasting, travelling, and getting married. There is a right time for everything, and determining when is the job of the astrologer.

Because of the differences between the Hindu and Gregorian calendars it is impossible to give exact dates for festivals, although it is possible to give a rough guideline. Not all of them are celebrated by every Hindu—some have a special regional meaning; others are kept only by devotees of a particular deity. Some festivals are family-based; others are occasions when temple-visiting and pilgrimage are popular.

In addition to annual festivals, there are some rituals which take place on a monthly or weekly basis, including fasts to particular deities, such as the monthly *Ekadashi* during which Krishna is petitioned, and each Friday when the Goddess is worshipped. Also important are fairs (*mela*), life-cycle rites (*samskara*), and

Box 2 Major Hindu festivals

Divali, Deepavali (October/November): Festival of lights. Lasting several days, it is variously associated with the gods Rama and Krishna and the goddess Lakshmi. Small lamps are lit and presents are often given.

Makar Sankranti, Pongal, Lohri (January): *Makar Sankranti* means 'entry into Capricorn'. It marks the end of the harvest and is celebrated with fireworks and sweets. It is celebrated as *Pongal* in Tamil Nadu, where rice is boiled and offered to the sun.

Shivaratri (February/March): Principal festival for *Shaiva* Hindus when offerings are made to Shiva and his praises are sung.

Holi (March): Festival often associated with the defeat of a demoness called Holika. Coloured powders or paint are often thrown in a spirit of merriment and mischief.

Ramnavmi (April): Celebration of the anniversary of Rama's birth, with readings of the *Ramayana*.

Ratha Yatra (June/July): 'Car festival', when Lord Jagannath (a form of Krishna) is pulled through the streets in a huge chariot in Puri, Orissa (and in some western cities with Hindu populations).

Raksha Bandhan (August): Festival which reinforces family relationships. Girls tie threads around their brothers' wrists in exchange for protection and a small gift.

Krishna Janamashtami (August/September): Principal festival for Krishna, celebrating his birth. The *Bhagavata Purana* is often read.

Onam (August/September): Harvest festival in Kerala, with traditional snake-boat races.

Ganesh Chaturthi (September): Festival celebrating the god Ganesha, particularly important among Maharastrians.

Navaratri, Durga Puja (September/October): Festival for the Goddess. *Navaratri* or 'nine nights' of folk dancing to worship Ambamata, celebrated by Gujaratis in India and abroad. Important in Bengal where elaborate images of Durga are worshipped.

Dashera, Dussehra (September/October): The 'tenth', the night following *Navaratri* when Rama's victory over Ravana is celebrated. In parts of north India, plays (*Ram-lila*) are performed which recount the story from the *Ramayana*.

national occasions such as *Vaisakhi* (a spring holiday celebrated on 13 April) and Republic Day (26 January). Deities are also honoured regularly in temple worship, and served through communal religious life.

Madurai, a temple city

This ancient temple city in Tamil Nadu is more than just a great place of worship. Its temple architecture and sculpture are themselves a testimony to the way in which earlier generations of Hindus sought to serve and praise their sovereign deities. Originally centred on a royal palace and the figure of the king, Madurai came under the influence of a growing devotional movement which took hold in the south of India. A large and prestigious temple city grew up there at a time when temples were being sponsored and erected throughout the region by ruling dynasties (from the 6th to the 9th century CE). The present structure is from a later period and shares some of the same features as other south Indian temples, with towering gateways (*gopuram*), laid out on a square plan, with a large tank for ritual bathing, and two principal temples each containing an inner sanctum under a golden tower (*shikara*) with halls and an antechamber. The sacred centre in each is referred to as 'the cave within the mountain', and within them reside the divine guests—in one, Minakshi, the royal queen and warrior-turned-goddess, and, in the other, her husband, Sundareshvara (a form of Shiva, residing in a *linga*).

It is Minakshi, not her husband, who is the principal deity of Madurai and she is sometimes worshipped on her own, although the festive occasion of her marriage to Sundareshvara is celebrated annually by more than 50,000 pilgrims. Each day, in public worship conducted by temple priests for the benefit of all, after being praised and showered with offerings, a portable image of Sundareshvara is brought ceremonially to the bedchamber of Minakshi, where the two deities are sung to and rocked in their swing before spending the night together behind closed doors.

On an ordinary day at the temple 20,000 to 25,000 visitors may pass through, attending the public *puja*, as well as performing their own devotions. They may also obtain the services of a priest to make offerings on their behalf and to recite the 108 names of the deity. These brahmin priests gain the right, purity, and power to serve Minakshi and Sundareshvara by virtue of being born into a particular caste and by undergoing rites of initiation and consecration. They serve the needs of the deities and are also the channels through which ordinary devotees make offerings and receive divine blessings.

ISKCON, a worshipping community

Hindus may also respond to the divine presence by accepting the refuge or shelter of a guru, and then becoming involved in his or her community. One example is the Hare Krishna movement that grew up around A. C. Bhaktivedanta Swami, a Bengali *sannyasi* who left India at the age of 69 to spread awareness and love of Krishna in the West. The organization he founded in America in 1966, the International Society for Krishna Consciousness (ISKCON), grew quickly until his death in 1977. It is now a global movement, with centres in many countries, including India.

Those who have met Hare Krishna devotees or bought their books may be familiar with two phrases which reflect their ideas about the divine/human relationship. Krishna is referred to as 'the supreme personality of god-head', indicating that he is the ultimate divine person. 'Back to god-head' (also the name of the Society's magazine) expresses the desire of the devotee to return home to his or her eternal relationship with Krishna. From the writings of Bhaktivedanta Swami, particularly his commentaries on the *Bhagavad-gita* and *Bhagavata Purana*, devotees learn to see all their actions as opportunities for divine service. This extends beyond worship in the temple to the private chanting of the Hare Krishna *mantra*, to singing the names of Krishna and preaching his glories, and to daily chores during which his name should be repeatedly remembered.

Devotees repeat, as their founder did, the plea of the 16th-century Bengali saint, Chaitanya, that the name of Krishna should be spread 'in every town and village'. To take this seriously means that devotees should not be content to respond to Krishna solely by improving their own spiritual discipline, but by exposing others to Krishna and the path of devotional service (*bhakti yoga*). Invitations are extended to people to visit temples and take *darshana*, to attend lectures, buy books, join festival programmes, and eat *prashada*, food blessed by Krishna. Public worship, processions, and pilgrimages take the name and form of Krishna on to the streets of India's villages and the cities of the West and beyond.

Like the widespread response to the miracle of Ganesha, such worship of Krishna is a global phenomenon, evidence that the presence of the divine in its Hindu forms now extends beyond India. The historical changes which paved the way for this to happen are the subject of Chapter 6.

Chapter 6
Hinduism, colonialism, and modernity

For you I live, O Allah-Rama.
Show mercy to your slave, my lord.
... And if God only lives in mosques,
whose land lies in between?
Can Ram reside in images and pilgrims' stops?
In neither one has he been seen.
The east is the abode of Hari;
Allah's station's in the West.
But Rama and Rahim both lie within my heart,
and there alone is where to seek them.
As many women, men, that have been born:
they're all your forms.
Allah-Rama's little child, Kabir
knows that one as his guru and his pir.

This is part of a poem entitled 'Warnings' by the 15th-century *bhakti* poet, Kabir. He lived in north India at a time when it was under Mughal control and when Islam was the religion of the rulers. His family, of the weaver's caste, had become Muslims, though their conversion may well have been more a matter of form than conviction. Kabir, at least, was disgusted by the outward practice of both Muslims and Hindus. He believed strongly that God—who was ultimately without form—manifested in the hearts of his devotees.

Ritual practices, images, symbols, and buildings were all unnecessary.

Kabir was just one of a great many Indian mystical poets who wrote lovingly in praise of God while criticizing social injustices and religious formalities. From the 6th century CE in southern India to the 18th century in Bengal, such poetry was spoken, sung, and written, with some poets expressing love of Vishnu or Krishna, others of Shiva or Devi, and those like Kabir (and Nanak, the first of the Sikh gurus), love of the supreme One without name or form. From before the time of Kabir and Chaitanya, the religion of the Hindus developed in the context of foreign rule, first the Delhi Sultanate (1211–1526) and Mughal empire (1526–1757), then the British Raj. I have chosen Kabir as an illustration because his words show the influence of both the religion indigenous to India and the religion of the conquerors.

In another poem, Kabir announced, 'Saints, I see the world is mad'. He believed that Hindus and Muslims had lost sight of the truth and taken refuge in irrelevancies, even resorting to religious antagonism and violence. He described a situation that was to continue beyond the period of Muslim rule to later centuries when Christianity, rather than Islam, was the religion of the rulers. Although neither the Mughals nor the British actually imposed their religion on the Indians, in general both eyed Hindu beliefs and practices with suspicion and saw their own religion as superior. There were exceptions to this: the 16th-century Mughal emperor Akbar was known for his deep interest in and tolerance of those of other religions, and the 18th-century British administrators who studied Hindu scriptures acquired a positive image of the religion of early India.

In such a brief introduction to Hinduism it is not possible to give a detailed history of the events which surrounded the presence of the Arabs and Turks, then the Europeans in India (see timeline for dates). What is of most importance here is the impact of such a presence on the religious ideas and practices of Hindus, and it is to this that I now turn, in particular to the effect of British colonialism.

The European discovery of Hinduism

Europeans traded with India for spices and textiles as early as the classical and medieval periods, though perhaps the best known trader was the Portuguese Vasco da Gama who arrived on the Malabar coast at the end of the 15th century in search of 'Christians and spices'. These two motives are indicative of what was to follow in later centuries: the European desire to see India in its own Christian image and judge it accordingly, and to benefit from its riches—its goods and its culture.

The arrival of the Portuguese was followed in the 16th and 17th centuries by the Dutch, British, and French, all of whom established trading companies. Of these, it was the British who strengthened their commercial and administrative position and came eventually to dominate India politically. From their base in Madras (now Chennai), the British East India Company secured Bengal by military force in 1757 and made Warren Hastings Governor-General in 1772. His period of office marked the intervention of the British Government in Indian affairs. Hastings is remembered as an administrator, but he was also important for his patronage of Sanskrit scholarship.

In this period, a number of books by Europeans were published about India and its religion. Many repeated the themes of earlier travel writing in which popular religion was abhorred and Hindu ethical and philosophical doctrines approved (though not always properly understood). From the 1770s, significant scholarly progress was made by men in the employ of the East India Company, most notably by Charles Wilkins, with the first English translation of the *Bhagavad-gita* (1785), and William Jones, with his *Asiatick Researches* (from 1789) including his translation of the *Manusmriti*. Both Sanskrit scholars presented the Hindu religion in a positive light, showing its antiquity and stressing the themes within it that a western audience could admire in their own terms. As Warren Hastings wrote in his recommendation of Wilkins's *Bhagvat-Geeta*,

> Every instance which brings their [the inhabitants of India] real character home to observation will impress us with a more generous sense of feeling for their natural rights, and teach us to estimate them by the measure of our own. But such instances can only be obtained in their writings: and these will survive when the British dominion in India shall have long ceased to exist, and when the sources which it once yielded of wealth and power are lost to remembrance.

While the Hindu scriptures were being brought to a new audience by such scholars—'orientalists' as they became known—a very different study of Indian religion was being undertaken by a rather unusual figure. Based in Madras and the Deccan rather than Bengal, a French Jesuit rather than a British administrator, Abbé Dubois toiled to collect information for a manuscript on *Hindu Manners, Customs, and Ceremonies*. Like Hastings, Wilkins, and Jones, he was aware of the ignorance of most Europeans and sought to rectify this with a detailed ethnographic account compiled through many years of intimate acquaintance with Hindus. He lived as they did, dressed like them, and gained their confidence. He was circumspect in avoiding 'any display of repugnance' towards their behaviour. His manuscript was translated into English in 1815, and quickly became a resource for those Europeans eager to form an opinion of the religious culture of India.

Christianity and reform Hinduism

Abbé Dubois's account was full of colourful detail about the caste arrangements, brahminical lifestyle, and religious practices of south Indian Hinduism, yet his purpose was not to commend, but to inform. As a Jesuit, he was eager to promote Christianity and felt it was only possible to do this once one had a deep knowledge of Indian society and culture: 'It struck me that a faithful picture of the wickedness and incongruities of polytheism and idolatry would by its very ugliness help greatly to set off the beauties and perfections of Christianity.' Those of a more evangelical persuasion—like the anti-slavery campaigner William Wilberforce—disagreed and preferred a more proactive approach to outlawing such practices and promoting Christianity, but many British administrators in India were wary of antagonizing the population and provoking civil unrest.

Although the East India Company only formally lifted its ban on missionary activity in its territories in 1813, a few zealous Christians had settled before this. A key figure was William Carey, a Baptist who went to India in 1793. With no official backing or sponsorship, he spent several years with his family in bitter poverty, travelling through Bengal before setting up the Serampore Mission with two other missionaries. He learnt Bengali and Sanskrit, translating the Bible into Bengali in 1800. As a proselytizer, he was largely unsuccessful, however, since very few Bengalis embraced Christianity. Elsewhere, where Hindus did convert, it was not the hoped-for brahmins, but the powerless and disenfranchized lower castes and untouchables who made the switch.

One Hindu brahmin who was known to the Serampore missionaries and was influenced by them was Ram Mohan Roy (1772–1833). With a command of Persian, Arabic, Greek, Latin, and English as well as Bengali and Sanskrit, and a knowledge of Islam and Christianity as well as his own Hindu religion, he was the first Indian to comment in print in English on the British, their religion, and its place in the Indian context. As a social reformer, he outraged orthodox Hindus by writing against idolatry, *sati*, child-marriage, and caste, and in favour of education for women. And, as a Hindu with new ideas, he was praised and criticized in turn by

Christians—praised for reading the New Testament, for his appreciation of the ethical teachings of Jesus, and his Unitarian sympathies, but criticized for his failure to accept Jesus as the son of God. Roy's reforming zeal was not confined to social issues. In 1828, he formed the Brahmo Samaj with like-minded friends in order to promote the reasoned, ethical monotheism which he believed to be rooted in the *Upanishads* and *Brahma Sutra*. Images of gods and goddesses and their worship were forbidden on Samaj premises. Looking back at this movement and the many writings of Ram Mohan Roy, it is possible to see the influence of both Islam and Christianity as well as *advaita vedanta* on his thought. Striking also is the way in which his ideas were disseminated. A truly modern Indian, he made use of all the novel means at his disposal, printing pamphlets, circulating newspapers, and petitioning for civil rights. Roy travelled to Britain in 1830 to represent the interests of the Mughal emperor, but died in Bristol just three years later having made firm friends with English Unitarians with whom he shared a belief in the oneness and unity of God. His place is now secured in local history by his mausoleum in Arnos Vale cemetery and a statue, erected in 1997, on Bristol's College Green.

Hinduism on the offensive

The reformist impulse of the Brahmo Samaj continued, particularly through the campaigning efforts of a later leader, Keshub Chandra Sen (1838–84), who pursued women's issues still further by calling for widows to be allowed to remarry. Other 19th-century figures made similar pleas. Dayananda Saraswati (1824–83), who founded the Arya Samaj in 1875, stressed the Vedic religious partnership between men and women and the importance of women's education. He and others looked back to the great debates of the *Upanishads* in which women had taken part.

The focus on 'women's uplift' was one aspect of the trend by orientalists and Hindu reformers to reclaim the Aryan past. The argument rested upon acceptance of the idea of a former great civilization which had gradually been eroded over the centuries by popular religious practices and social customs claimed by critics to be 'superstitious', 'idol-worship', 'polytheism', and 'caste abuse'. This argument became central to the Hindu nationalist cause, and was repeated not only by the Arya Samaj, but by later campaigners and movements (including those active today). It met with dissenters, however, who doubted the historical accuracy of the claim to an Aryan golden age and dismissed as divisive the favouring of Aryans above others.

Many of the new Hindu initiatives of the 19th century were pervaded to some extent by the influence of western culture and Christian values. Where Hindu leaders did not positively endorse these, they reacted against them: the Arya Samaj, for example, reconverted low-caste Hindus who had been drawn to Christianity. Many new groups mimicked the organizational and administrative practices and structures of British societies, and, like Ram Mohan Roy, they used the printed word as a means of spreading their ideas.

One Hindu who was arguably less shaped by colonial norms was Ramakrishna (1836–86). From a poor brahmin family, he had become a priest of the goddess Kali in the Dakshineshwara temple near Calcutta (now Kolkata). He developed a deep relationship with Mother Kali, whom he later saw present in his young wife, Sarada. He also embarked on an inner journey in which he learnt Tantric disciplines, experienced the oneness of the *advaita* vision, enjoyed love of Krishna, and explored Christian and Muslim spirituality. His profound insights and mystical behaviour impressed many people, particularly a young British-educated sceptic, Narendranath Datta (1863–1902). Later taking the name Vivekananda, it was this devotee who was to give ideological and institutional shape to his guru's vision (see Box 3). However, as an embodiment of the goddess, it was Sarada Devi who was to provide a spiritual focus for many of her husband's devotees.

Box 3 Vivekananda's achievements

1880s	Narendranath Datta was a member of the Brahmo Samaj
1881	Met Ramakrishna
1886	Death of Ramakrishna; Ramakrishna Order established
1886–92	Travelled as a *sannyasi* (with the spiritual name of Vivekananda) of the Ramakrishna Order. Decisive spiritual insights at Cape Comorin (now Kanyakumari)
1893	Attended the World Parliament of Religions in Chicago
1893–6	Lecture tour of the USA and brief visit to England. (Main topics of lectures: Hinduism, especially *advaita vedanta*; East–West understanding; Indian social conditions)
1894	First Vedanta Society founded in New York
1896	Returned to India
1897	Ramakrishna Mission founded in India, with a focus on social reform
1899	Brief return to the USA
1902	Death of Vivekananda

A religious organization for women—the Ramakrishna Sarada Math and Mission—was formally established in 1954 in Sarada Devi's name. Now also active in South Africa and Australia, it has some twenty branches in India at which women may study and live. It offers initiation to women according to vows endorsed by the orthodox *Shankara-acharya* tradition. It is one of only a few movements which endorses women's renunciation of the world and allows them to become *sannyasinis*.

From India to the West and back again

Vivekananda's chief contribution was in presenting contemporary Hindu teachings to the West, for the West. The 20th-century western understanding of Hinduism before the 1970s was formed largely by Vivekananda and reflected the monistic vision he referred to simply as 'Vedanta'. Vedanta Societies grew up in a number of American cities, drawing in many people disillusioned with Christianity and keen to experiment with new philosophical ideas.

When Vivekananda arrived in the West, many Americans were open to his message. In the 1840s and 1850s, several poets had expressed ideas akin to the teaching on *brahman* in the early *Upanishads*. Ralph Waldo Emerson and Henry David Thoreau, influenced by the translations of British orientalist William Jones, had published essays on Hindu scriptures in a journal called *The Dial*. Walt Whitman, in his collection *Leaves of Grass*, had poetically expressed a philosophy which some said was similar to Krishna's teaching in the *Bhagavad-gita*. These 'transcendentalist' poets were typical of many romantics who viewed India and her religion from afar. They imagined the East to be everything the West was not: mystical, mythical, ritualistic, symbolic; not materialistic, rational, or scientific. They were spiritual seekers, as were the two people who later formed the Theosophical Society in New York in 1875. Madame Helena Blavatsky and Colonel H. S. Olcott began a movement with occult leanings and an interest in Hindu and Buddhist thought—especially *karma* and reincarnation. The Theosophical Society remained popular in the West, but also took its message eastward, settling outside Madras in 1882. Its exponents, particularly an English woman named Annie Besant (who later became leader of the Indian National Congress), preached the wonders of Hinduism, defending it against missionary criticism and evoking pride in their heritage among Indian Hindus. Both Vivekananda and the Theosophical Society showed how ideas about Hinduism, fermented in the West, returned to India only to influence Hindus there.

Scholars of reform Hinduism, particularly Agehananda Bharati, referred to this process as the 'pizza effect'. The pizza, originally a type of plain bread, went with Italian migrants to America in the 19th century. There it developed into what we know today: flat bread topped with tomatoes, cheese, and anything else that might take the eater's fancy. Successful Italian-Americans returning to Italy to visit their families took with them the new-look pizza, which established itself in the homeland before being exported elsewhere as genuinely Italian. The export of an item, idea, or symbol, its cultural transformation, subsequent re-importation, and impact has been likened to this return journey of the pizza. The use of this metaphor in relation to reform Hinduism has been discussed and criticized in the 21st century, especially by Rajiv Malhotra who has argued for Hinduism's philosophical unity against ideas about its cultural and ideological diversity.

A further example of the dynamism of reform Hinduism can be seen with Mohandas K. Gandhi (1869–1948). A Gujarati Hindu nurtured in Vaishnavism, Gandhi was exposed to the Jain ideas of the region of his birth. He went to London in the 1880s to study law. Leaving sacred India (*bharat*) and going to the land of the foreigners was a momentous step for which he was ejected from the *bania* trading caste (though later ritually reinstated). Once settled, he sought out people with whom he could share his cultural traditions—free-thinking vegetarians and theosophists. It was with them that he read the *Bhagavad-gita* for the first time, as well as Sir Edwin Arnold's *The Light of Asia* (on the Buddha) and the New Testament.

The *Bhagavad-gita*—which he read in English—was to influence Gandhi deeply throughout his life. It fuelled his thinking on non-attachment and the way of action (*karma yoga*), ideas which became important in his non-violent resistance to the British and his campaign for Indian self-rule. Gandhi's return to his spiritual roots was not without critical reflection, however. He accepted the four social categories of *varna*, but rejected untouchability; he upheld the traditional 'Sita' role for women, but argued for their rights. A cornerstone of his principles was *satyagraha*, holding fast to the truth, on which his political action was built. The one truth which lay at the heart of everything issued forth in an ethical and non-violent force for good.

Like the other Hindu reformers discussed here, Gandhi was committed to social reform and the reshaping of modern India with reference to her valuable spiritual traditions. He too developed his ideas and actions as one of the colonized in the context of British rule, sometimes imitating, sometimes resisting, but always influenced by western conceptions of India and Hinduism.

Suttee or *sati*? A heated debate

As 'widow-burning', 'suttee' had been condemned by the British and French as inhumane. Accounts of it by 19th-century travellers had alerted compatriots back home in Europe to its horrors. The etching from the missionary account of James Peggs depicts two European observers turning away from the scene and aggressive Indians wielding swords and fanning the flames (see Figure 7). The burning woman is presented as a passive, appealing victim.

7. An etching of *sati* from *India's Cries to British Humanity* by James Peggs, 1832.

Yet *sati* was not understood in this way by those Hindus who condoned it, or even those who sought its reform. *Sati* meant, in fact, 'a good woman', a devoted wife who chose to overcome death by becoming a goddess or *sati-mata*. Although the practice was not widespread, it occurred with some regularity in north India in the 18th century where it was considered an appropriate choice for high-caste women whose husbands died before them. However, while many orthodox Hindus supported it, there were others who despised it, most notably Ram Mohan Roy who campaigned vigorously for its abolition. The British, who were loath to interfere in Hindu religious affairs, were cautious, but eventually passed an Act in 1829 prohibiting it.

It is not easy to legislate against popular beliefs and practices, however, and instances of women's self-immolation have continued, albeit infrequently, since then. In 1987, in the village of Deorala in Rajasthan, a young wife named Roop Kanwar died on her husband's funeral pyre, and *sati* again became a contentious issue. Defended by her family, other local people, and many Hindu leaders, Roop's action was said to be her own choice. But many women in India asked, 'What woman would choose to die such a death?' Could this really have been a free choice, or was Roop pressurized into mounting the pyre? Pro-*sati* Hindus claimed that these critics were secularist detractors, influenced by western colonial animosity; those against *sati* denied they were anti-Hindu, asserting rather that they despised a practice which was oppressive of women and which had no significant scriptural sanction. The 1988 Sati Prevention Act criminalized the aiding, abetting, and glorifying of *sati*, but occasional cases continue to hit the media headlines.

Chapter 7
Challenges to Hinduism: women and *dalits*

In the mid-1970s and then again from 1980 until her assassination in 1984, Indira Gandhi was India's prime minister. Some years later, the Indian president was a man deemed to be of very low social status, a *dalit* or untouchable, K. R. Narayanan. Did their attainment of high office suggest that, by the end of the 20th century, women and *dalits* had achieved equality with other groups in Indian society? And, turning the spotlight on religion, could a woman or *dalit* now be appointed *Shankara-acharya* (see Chapter 2), the most revered role within orthodox Hinduism?

Are issues of status, hierarchy, and power in India related to Hindu ideas about how society should be ordered, organized, and led? Is it possible to separate social and religious questions or are they inextricably linked? As this chapter will show, such a distinction would be artificial and unworkable. In India, caste and gender issues are not simply social matters demanding a secular response; they are underpinned by religious ideas and maintained by customary practices and brahminical institutions. Arguably, the very nature of Hinduism as a religion, and even 'religion' itself, is challenged by this interrelationship.

Caste and gender: who is a Hindu?

In earlier chapters I described the institutions of *varna* and *jati*, and the important idea of *dharma*, order and duty, and its meaning for different social groups. An important text to discuss these was *Manusmriti* or the Laws of Manu. Composed around 200 BCE, chiefly with the interests of the brahmin community in mind, it made reference to non-brahmins, including low-caste *sudras* and those outside the *varna* system, which it referred to as *chandalas*. Both groups—and women too—were prohibited from hearing the *Veda*, from taking initiation and wearing the sacred thread. Of *chandalas*, Manu was dismissive, referring to them as 'dog-cookers' to denote their lowly status and impurity, barring them from owning property, and consigning them to dwell outside the village and perform its most demeaning tasks (sweeping, working with leather, and removing excrement and the dead). The touch of such a person was declared to be polluting to one of a higher group, and required ritual purification. Brahmins, the purest of all, had most to fear from the presence of *chandalas*, even though they needed them to undertake those very tasks that would endanger their status.

Also polluting was a menstruating woman. Her touch would require a brahmin to bathe. High-caste women, Manu said, should be under the protection of fathers, husbands, and then sons. They should never be independent, owing to their weak, fickle nature and the social consequences of allowing women to act outside male authority. A man must honour his wife, however, though he must also control her, by force if necessary, and keep her focused on her domestic duties. Bearing children—particularly sons—was her virtue. A good wife should serve even a bad husband as god. She should not leave him and, once widowed, she should not remarry. By Manu's time all women were prohibited from hearing the *Veda* and they were denied the opportunity of renouncing the world (*sannyasa*).

Manu's prescriptions were intended for women of twice-born classes, and not for those of lower status. However, the norms and expectations arising from them (for example, submissiveness to the wishes of the husband and his family, tolerance of abuse, preference for sons, and restricted freedom) pervaded Hindu society more generally, affecting how all women felt they should behave and how others viewed them. Women were not marginalized to the same extent as *chandalas*, but they had no direct access to religious scriptures and institutions or to spiritual progress and a relationship with the divine.

If this was the theory, what about the practice? There are few descriptive accounts available of Hindu life in India before the 19th century, so little is known of the actual experience of these two groups. The *bhakti* movement, however, was innovative in allowing previously excluded people to express their devotion. Women poets like Antal, Akkamahadevi, and Mirabai, and low-caste poets, including Kabir and the leather-worker Ravidas, showed that love of God was open to all, irrespective of gender or caste, and that it could be expressed openly in one's mother tongue. Barred from hearing the Sanskrit *Veda* and from access to the religion of the twice-born, they discovered their own spiritual path, an intimate and direct relationship with their Lord (see Figure 8).

It was not until the 20th century, however, that large numbers of women and untouchables became involved in voicing their own views and shaping the debates on gender and caste.

The women's movement

As Chapter 6 made plain, the situation of women and the problem of caste were important to colonialists and Hindu reformers because they were held to be a mark of India's religious and social decline. From the 1880s, middle-class women became increasingly involved in professional life and the movement for reform, though

8. A woman worshipping at a Shiva *linga*, from the Manley *Ragamala*, *c*.1610.

progress was slow and difficult. One of the most committed women of this period was Pandita Ramabai (1858–1922), who campaigned publicly for the education of child-widows, women's admission to medical colleges, and the training of teachers. She wrote *The High Caste Hindu Woman* in 1887 and founded a residential school for young widows in 1889. She came from a brahmin family, but her disenchantment with the lack of opportunities for women within the Hindu reform and revival movement contributed to her decision to convert to Christianity, for which she was ostracized by Bengali Hindus. She was joined by other women in her call for women's education, their argument being that, as 'mothers of the nation', women should be adequately trained. Sarojini Naidu (1879–1926), a future leader of the women's movement and Indian National Congress, said: 'Educate your women and the nation will take care of itself... the hand that rocks the cradle rules the world.' Women's involvement in nationalism grew with their calls for education, and both Annie Besant and Sarojini Naidu drew on Hindu goddesses and women in Hindu mythology to provide role models for women and their involvement in political struggle.

This activism continued from the 1920s to Indian independence in 1947, and women joined with men in campaigns for civil disobedience organized by Gandhi in his pursuit of Indian self-rule. They fought to be allowed to participate in the salt march of 1930 to demonstrate against the salt tax imposed by the British, and were then made leaders of many of the groups set up to break the salt laws, boycott the use of foreign cloth, develop home industries, and arrange pickets and demonstrations. Many women were arrested for their participation in such actions.

Once the independence of India was achieved, women were once again able to focus on gaining equality and rights. They were hopeful that the new Government would enshrine these within the Constitution and a new Hindu Code Bill. Equality was indeed guaranteed in the Constitution of 1950, but their hopes regarding the raising of the age of consent and marriage, women's right to divorce, and changes to the laws on inheritance and dowry did not materialize in a new Bill (though some were later introduced in separate Acts).

It was not until the 1970s and 1980s, however, that campaigning for rights spread from the few, educated voices of politically aware women to the grassroots, with agitation growing around the country *for* workers' rights for women, improvements to inheritance laws, environmental protection, and a common civil code, and *against* dowry and its abuse, domestic violence, rape, and *sati*. An all-India women's association had first been formed in 1917, but it was the 1970s and 1980s that saw the coming of age of the movement for women with groups forming in cities, towns, and villages to deal with local concerns, and with women from all social and religious strata willing to speak and act publicly. The setting up in 1978 of *Manushi*, a journal for women by women (co-edited by Madhu Kishwar and Ruth Vanita), provided the opportunity to reappraise women's situation, their roles, images, and visions. In this, as in many other initiatives, women worked together, aware of their common interests as well as different starting points. They protested against the rise of communalism, in which the different religious and political agendas of Hindus, Muslims, and Sikhs came increasingly into conflict, and which threatened the efforts of the women's movement to make gains for all women irrespective of background.

Daughters, dowry, and sex determination

Even before the composition of the *Manusmriti*, Vedic society was male-dominated with men heading the household and inheriting property. It was the *dharma* of women to give birth to sons: 'The birth of a girl, grant it elsewhere. Here grant a son' (*Atharva Veda* 3, 23). This idea persists, as this women's prayer shows: 'May houses be full of daughters-in-law but very few daughters; may they see the faces of grandsons and great-grandsons.' Many autobiographical accounts by Indian women also confirm this sense that a daughter's birth is not always welcome. The failure to produce a son is often seen as a punishment for misconduct in a previous life, with unhappy consequences for the here and now. Not only are sons the ones who by tradition support the family and conduct rituals at the death of their parents, but they also bring wealth into the family at the time of marriage. Daughters, however, are a drain on the family's resources, as money and goods (dowry) have to be given by her parents to the groom and his family when they marry.

Dowry was prohibited in an Act of 1961, but what was once confined to higher caste communities is now a widespread and growing practice, with the costs of marrying a daughter rising annually. And, although both men and women claim to be against it, the practice continues ('Rising number of dowry deaths in India', *The Hindu*, 7 August 2013). Of still greater concern is the abuse of wives which is associated with it. Demands, which are often violently enforced, are frequently made by husbands and in-laws for more money and goods after the marriage. Deaths are not infrequent. Young wives are murdered—usually by burning—so that a husband is free to remarry to obtain another dowry, and all too often women commit suicide because of incessant abuse: 'Housewife dies of burns: kin cry foul' (*The Times of India*, 9 August 2010); 'Harassed for dowry; housewife ends life' (*The Deccan Herald*, 15 December 2014).

Since the end of the 1970s many women and men have campaigned actively against dowry in India and beyond. Some families have refused to participate in the giving or taking of dowry, an idea encouraged by a number of religious groups. The law on dowry in India was amended in 1983, and some abusers have since been imprisoned, but distinguishing between a kitchen accident and a dowry murder has proved difficult for the police and the courts.

Imagine the anxiety, then, of parents with daughters and no sons. How is the money to be raised for their dowries, and, once married, will they become the victims of such abuse? It is in the context of such fears that some would-be-parents, those who can afford an amniocentesis test and an abortion if necessary, resort to sex selection despite it being illegal. So deep-rooted is the problem that, in 2015, India's Supreme Court ordered online search sites, including Google and Yahoo, to block advertisements offering foetal sex determination. Despite public awareness campaigns and doctors vowing never to reveal the sex of a foetus, the problem continues, with the Census of India 2011 revealing a worsening child sex ratio (from 104.0 males to every 100 females in 1981 to 108.8 males to 100 females in 2011).

What questions do these human rights abuses pose for Hinduism? Are they addressed by contemporary Hindu groups? How do such groups respond to the deep-seated bias towards sons within Hindu tradition? To what extent do Hindu women believe that their religion can be reformed to recognize their value and interests? Have some decided, like Pandita Ramabai, that traditional and reform groups offer no hope and looked instead for spiritual alternatives, either in other religions or in new spiritual initiatives?

Ambedkar: what path freedom?

Unlike those reformers who spoke out against caste and hoped for a moral revolution within Hinduism which would bring about the spiritual equality of untouchables, Dr B. R. Ambedkar (1891–1956) adopted a more radical position and called for legal change. He was an untouchable himself, though an unusual one for his time. After higher education at Columbia University, New York, and the London School of Economics, he returned to India and became involved in national politics, taking part in pre-independence negotations with the British and, after 1947, assuming a leading role in the constitutional drafting committee.

His interests lay in what he referred to as the material and spiritual conversion of the untouchables, the former leading him to work for social democracy, rights for landless labourers, and the criminalization of offences against untouchables. In pressing for their spiritual conversion, Ambedkar first analysed the contribution of Hindu teachings to the plight of untouchables. There was no equality in Hinduism, and no place for individual progress or judgement, he said. 'I tell you all very specifically, religion is for man and not man for religion. To get human treatment, convert yourselves... Convert for securing equality. Convert for getting liberty... Why do you remain in that religion which prohibits you from entering a temple... from drinking water from a public well? Why do you remain in that religion which insults you at every step?'

Having declared as early as 1935 his intention not to die a Hindu, Ambedkar, with half a million followers, rejected his religious past and publicly embraced Buddhism in 1956, thus offering untouchables a new religious identity, one which accepted the existence of suffering yet taught a path to its cessation through individual effort.

Untouchability and the rise of *dalit* identity

Like abuse of women, crimes against untouchables are all too frequently reported in India's newspapers. Those the Government designated 'Scheduled Castes' and Gandhi named *Harijans* (children of God), together with Indian tribal peoples, make up nearly one-fifth of the Indian population, most living in India's villages as landless agricultural labourers, with many bonded to those of higher castes. Despite their number, their equality with other Indians in the Constitution, and the legislation designed to protect them (the Untouchability Offences Act of 1955 and Scheduled Caste and Scheduled Tribe (Prevention of Atrocities) Act of 1990), they are frequently the victims of violence, rape, and individual or mass murder, and continue to be denied their rights (to education, entry to temples, freedom of residence, and the use of wells). Government policies which have reserved places for them in education and government service have enraged some higher caste Hindus who have to compete for places, and violence has often followed. The number of crimes against scheduled castes increased rapidly from 1981 to 2001 (from 14,318 to 33,501), with the incidence levelling off but not declining in subsequent years.

Like women, the large untouchable minority is not a homogeneous group, but is divided by caste, tribe, and language. Internal differences have made joint action difficult, but, by the 1970s, a new and distinct identity was beginning to emerge from the activities of writers and small grassroots groups throughout India. Their focus was on their common experience of exclusion as *dalits*; those who were 'broken', 'scattered', and 'oppressed'. Through the literature and performance of protest, newspapers and journals such as *The Dalit Voice*, local acts of resistance, and interventions by Scheduled Caste and Scheduled Tribe MPs in political debate, *dalits* and tribal Indians (*adivasis*) began to act together and make their voices heard. Their leaders called for *dalits* to embrace secular humanism as a moral creed based on the present well-being of humanity, and to reject the divisive hierarchical laws and duties associated with orthodox Hinduism and the other-worldly focus of religion in general. *Dalit* thinking was 'counter-cultural', the objective being to claim an alternative history and identity not bound by the dominant ideology of brahminical Hinduism, but which might offer a way forward to a more just and open future. As the Gujarati *dalit* poet Neerav Patel wrote in 'Burning at Both the Ends',

> we can love each other
> if you can shed your orthodox skin.
> come and touch, we will make a new world—
> where there won't be any
> dust, dirt, poverty, injustice and oppression.

Religion and protest

Many people in the modern *dalit* and women's movements have turned from Hindu to secular answers in the hope of attaining equality and justice. There were great hopes that, after Indian independence, the secular Government of India would effect change for both groups through the law. Such change has been disappointingly slow and, even when new Acts were brought in, they proved difficult to enforce against the weight of religious and social tradition and the force of vested interests.

Secularism has not been the only haven for oppressed groups, however. As we have seen, in the centuries before it became an option, women and low-caste people found that the path of *bhakti* offered them self-esteem and an opportunity for liberation. Tantric and *Shaiva* movements were more accommodating than *Vaishnava* ones, particularly in the south, where the challenge to brahminical orthodoxy was strongest. Non-indigenous religions also had an appeal, particularly for those from low castes. Kabir's family, as noted in Chapter 6, had converted to Islam. In the 19th century some untouchables responded to the missionary pressures of Christianity, evoking a strong reaction from Hindu revivalist and nationalist movements, which began their own campaigns of outreach to those from low castes. Even today, around 80 per cent of India's Christians are from excluded communities.

Embracing a new religious identity which offers equality and liberation, and denying the old with its inherent injustices, has been an important strategy for *dalits*. Some followed the lead of Ambedkar into Buddhism, and others became Sikhs. But these other religions have not always offered an adequate answer to their needs. Those who converted to Sikhism, for example, were referred to as *Mazhbi Sikhs*, and were clearly distinguished from those of higher castes. As a result, *dalits* have begun to form their own religious communities, reclaiming religious figures and symbols which they believe can affirm their humanity and liberate them from oppression. Different groups of Punjabi *dalits* have come to associate themselves with Valmiki (the renowned storyteller of the *Ramayana*) and to revere Ravidas (the untouchable *bhakti* poet), and religious organizations have grown up around them.

Inverting Hindu symbols and traditions as a form of protest is not new. For centuries in south India, those outside the top castes have asserted a subversive Dravidian, low-caste identity by telling the *Ramayana* story with Ravana as hero and Rama (who signifies the north Indian, brahminical worldview) as villain. Rural women, too (see Chapter 4), have their own versions of the story which run counter to more orthodox renditions.

But women's religious protest has at times been different to that of the *dalits* because of their situation within Hindu society, particularly within the family. They are separated from one another by their positions as daughter, daughter-in-law, mother, and mother-in-law. Nevertheless, the songs they sing and stories they tell within the family often provide space to overturn the status quo, to complain and mock. And in their rituals, which do not require the presence of a brahmin, women are the experts. They have their own ways of exercising spiritual agency (see Figure 9).

Hindu reform movements established by and for women, such as the Order developed in memory of Sarada Devi, often challenged women's place in the Hindu family by encouraging women to leave and to live as students or renouncers. The Brahma Kumari movement, founded by a man called Dada Lekhraj in the 1930s, came into conflict with the families of its early women members because it encouraged chastity and asexual love. Brahma Kumaris do not protest vocally against the sexual and physical abuse of women within the family, but they offer an alternative, seeking a gradual transformation of family relationships through *yoga* and abstention from alcohol and sex.

9. *Sati* handprints: a memorial to women immolated on their husbands' funeral pyres.

Religious protest by women and *dalits* has taken many forms, from the pursuit of religious and secular alternatives to remaining within a Hindu framework while seeking to reclaim its symbols, undermine its structures, or transform its traditions. To return to the question asked at the beginning of the chapter, it remains unlikely that either a woman or a *dalit* could be accepted in the traditional role of *Shankara-acharya*, but the issue of spiritual and material equality is certainly on the agenda, not only for women and *dalits* themselves, but among mainstream Hindu religious bodies. A major step was taken in August 2014, for example, when the Pandharpur temple in Maharastra accepted five men from scheduled castes and two women to serve as priests alongside Brahmins.

But this issue raises a problem for Hindu *dharma* as expressed in orthodox texts like the *Manusmriti*. Can widespread equality ever be fully achieved without a radical transformation of Hindu teachings on purity and pollution, and on the nature and duty of women and untouchables?

Chapter 8
Crossing the black waters: Hinduism beyond India

The boundaries of Hinduism have been challenged by the voices of low-caste people and women's groups, but their location and stability have also been called into question by the emigration of Hindus and the export of Hindu spirituality (see Map 2).

Scholars who have classified and typologized religions and their various dimensions have tended to see Hinduism as an *ethnic* religion, a religion of a particular people, one associated with their land or place. According to this view, a person is a Hindu by virtue of his or her birth within an Indian Hindu caste. Such a person, by tradition, was then subject to the *dharma* of his or her community, its rules and customs. The realm of *dharma*, the Hindu universe, was known as *bharat*, the land ritually purified by the brahmin and surrounded by *kala pani*, the black waters.

Historically, Buddhists, Christians, and Muslims have spread their religious ideas and practices by conversion and conquest. They are now found as majority populations in many different countries. Nearly all the world's Hindus, however, continue to live in the secular state of India, where they represent about 78 per cent of a population of nearly 1.3 billion, and Nepal, where Hinduism is the state religion and where 81 per cent of Nepalese are Hindu. This seems to lend strong support to the idea that Hinduism is an

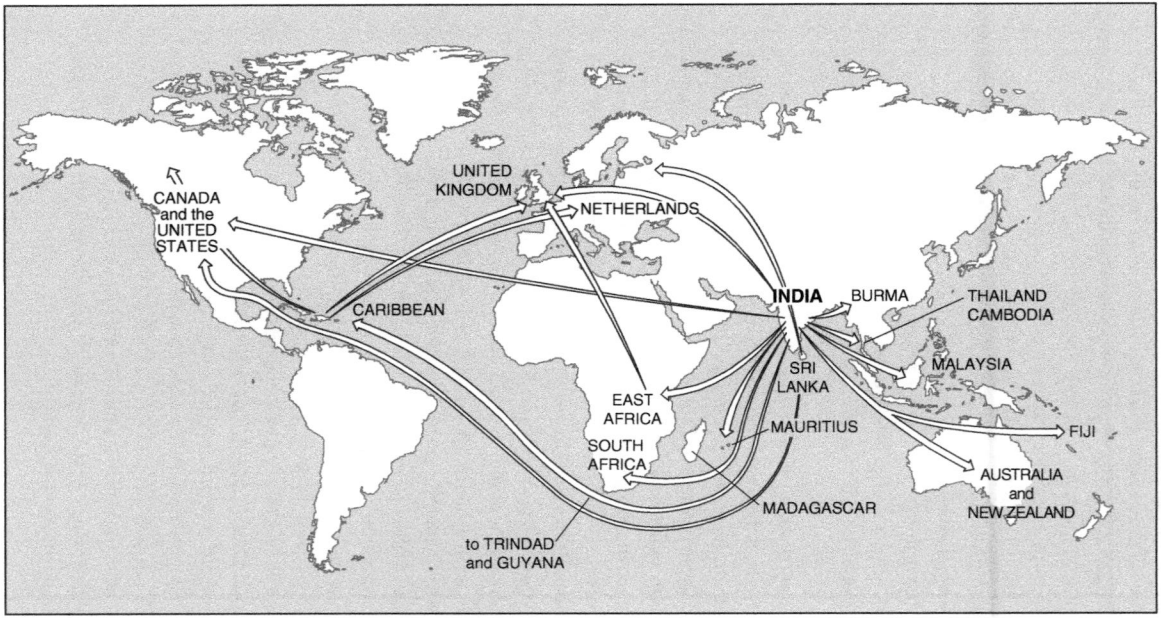

Map 2. Hindu migrations from India.

ethnic religion rather than a universalizing religion with a message for all, regardless of birth and location.

However, throughout the history of *bharat*, the sacred land now known as India, there have been those—like Gandhi and Ambedkar—who have left her shores for education, trade, or a profession, to settle or to work and then return home. How have they justified and managed their journey and period of residence across the black waters? One instructive story is told by an anthropologist, Richard Burghart, in *Hinduism in Great Britain*:

> In 1902 Madho Singh, Maharaja of Jaipur, was invited to London to attend the coronation of Edward VII. It was fitting that Madho Singh attend the ceremony, for Edward was Emperor of India and the Jaipur ruler owed him allegiance. Yet the Hindu king was filled with apprehension at the prospect of crossing the ocean and accepting British hospitality. To him, Great Britain was a remote, barbarous country, situated in the northwestern sector of the inauspicious 'Black Sea'. Madho Singh could not sustain his sacred person in such an alien environment. And such a journey would put his subjects at risk, for in the course of his coronation the people of Jaipur had been ritually constituted within the body of the king. Were Madho Singh to become personally defiled by his journey, his land and people would also become defiled. Thus Madho Singh faced a dilemma. He could travel to Great Britain, but only on condition that he did not leave India. He eventually found a way round his problem by chartering a ship, the S.S. *Olympia*, having the vessel cleansed throughout and ritually consecrated by the royal priest of Jaipur. Rice, dried fruit, vegetables, and water were brought on board, together with cows and fodder so that fresh milk could be supplied daily. Earth from the Sacred Land of the Hindus (*bharatavarsha*) and water from the Ganges were put in storage so that he could perform his daily ablutions and purify his alien surroundings. In this auspicious environment Madho Singh was safely conveyed to Britain.

As Burghart goes on to point out, however, Madho Singh was not the first Hindu to face this problem. In the early centuries CE brahmins travelled into south-east Asia (to what is now Cambodia, Thailand, and Bali) at the invitation of local rulers to consecrate their kingdoms. They remained, marrying local women, extending the ritual boundary of the sacred territory of *bharat*, and establishing aspects of brahminical culture such as their deities and scriptures. Today, in Thailand, the historical importance of the god Brahma is still witnessed in the Dheva Satarn temple in Bangkok and in royal ceremonies. The *Ramayana*, or *Ramakien* as it is known locally, remains significant in popular cultural performance. Despite such a heritage, these countries today are no little Indias, and those brahmins who continue to live and practise there as Hindu specialists are now fully Thai or Balinese.

Quite different has been the movement of merchants to other nearby countries for business. The Chettyars, a Tamil banking community, extended their business to Burma, Malaya (now Malaysia), Mauritius, and other parts of south-east Asia. Additionally, strong trading links have existed for many centuries between western India and East Africa. In the first decades of the 20th century Gujarati and Punjabi migrants (Sikhs and Muslims as well as Hindus), attracted by the opportunities available to work under the British administration on the new railroads and as small traders, set themselves up in the growing towns and cities of Kenya, Uganda, Tanganyika (now Tanzania), and Nyasaland (now Malawi).

The majority of these migrants were merchants and artisans rather than brahmins. Initially, they were content to leave regular religious duties to their families back home. Later, when they became more settled and were joined by relatives, they began to establish social and religious institutions for mutual support, education, cultural activities, and religious nurture. Gurus and swamis crossed the seas to visit these communities and encourage their religious practices. They consecrated new temples and held festivals and other devotional meetings.

Although the countries of East Africa, like India herself, were colonized by the British, Hindus and Indians of other religious persuasions travelled there freely in search of work and financial gain. They were able to maintain links with the homeland. Not so fortunate were those indentured by the British and Dutch after the abolition of slavery in the mid-19th century and transported to the plantations of Trinidad, British Guiana (now Guyana), Dutch Guiana (now Surinam), Fiji, Mauritius, and South Africa. Although promised the possibility of return to India, few were able to do so, with most settling in their new countries and eventually gaining their independence and the right to acquire land. The Hindu communities which grew up in these countries developed quite differently from one another, depending on factors such as their ethnic and caste composition, their relative size compared to other local communities, the impact upon them of indigenous religious, social, and political institutions, and their ability to acquire power and status.

An informative study of one country in which indentured Indian Hindus settled is *Hindu Trinidad* by Steven Vertovec. He depicts the lively devotional life of the Hindus, the musical renditions of the *Ramayana* that were popular in the 1960s and the grand, week-long *yajnas* (sacrificial rites) which were sponsored by families made newly rich in the oil boom of the 1970s and 1980s. He also mentions the brahmins who migrated with the indentured labourers to serve their religious needs, and the way in which regional and family traditions such as the worship of Kali often gave way to rituals endorsed by the brahmins. He ends with the demands of young Hindus for a vigorous and confident public Hindu identity able to compete successfully with the identities of other aspiring groups in Trinidad.

With indentured Hindus arriving from 1845, Hinduism in Trinidad has now been establishing itself for over 170 years. The arrival of Hindus in Europe and North America is a more recent phenomenon, with differing colonial traditions and immigration policies leading to variable patterns of settlement and community type. Comparing the Hindu migration to Britain and the United States, for example, reveals that settlement began earlier in the former as a result of Britain's colonial relationship with India. Many Hindus, as British passport-holders, arrived in Britain from East Africa in the 1960s and early 1970s as a result of nation-building policies in the newly independent states. In the USA, however, they came directly from India as professionals, entering to take up jobs in healthcare, education, and business. Since the 1980s, the range of countries of settlement increased still further as Tamil Hindu refugees fled civil war in Sri Lanka, with new communities developing, for example, in France, Germany, Switzerland, Norway, and Toronto, Canada. Hindus in the West in general have achieved a very high educational level and good standard of living, though many have also experienced discrimination and racism.

Interesting issues are raised about the nature of Hinduism as a religion by the growth of the Hindu diaspora (by 2012 Hindus were resident in 101 countries, see Box 4). The concept of 'diaspora' referred originally to Jews living in exile outside Judaea. Today it is used more generally to mean those populations living outside their land of origin, some of whom may be refugees who have been forced to leave their homes, whilst others may be migrants who have chosen to move for economic reasons.

Hindu communities outside India have been composed of people with many different motives for leaving India, but generally they have retained a common religious consciousness which connects them with India, their families and places of origin. They have shown themselves to be resourceful and flexible people able to live, work, and create communities in many, quite different settings. They have been prepared to contravene, or at least to

Box 4 Hindus outside India: population statistics

Hindus make up approximately 15 per cent of the world's population. However, there are no precise figures for the total number of Hindus living outside India. The major reason is that many countries do not keep statistics for religious adherence. The figures given below are estimates, taken from a variety of sources.

Country	Number of Hindus	% of population
India	995,000,000	78.3
Nepal	23,410,450	81.3
Bangladesh	18,665,594	12.4
Sri Lanka	3,138,947	12.1
Pakistan	9,000,000	3.3
Indonesia	4,693,880	1.7
Malaysia	1,630,000	7.0
Fiji	303,163	33.0
Mauritius	625,441	48.5
Philippines	2,000,000	2.0
South Africa	959,000	1.9
Kenya	369,137	1.0
Tanzania	354,458	0.9
Trinidad and Tobago	237,737	22.5
Guyana	253,801	33.0
Suriname	94,157	20.0
United Kingdom	832,000	1.7
Canada	497,200	1.6
United States	1,204,560	0.5
United Arab Emirates	944,352	21.2

These figures provide a snapshot of the world Hindu population at one point in time (2012), but they are not able to reflect historical changes. For example, the Hindu population of what is now Bangladesh and Pakistan was much higher before the partition of India in 1947. Uganda, not listed above, had a population of 65,000 Hindus in 1970, but every one of them was expelled a few years later by Idi Amin. In recent decades a growing number have returned to live and work there.

There are also sizeable Hindu populations in countries not listed—Singapore, Oman, Qatar, Australia, New Zealand, Thailand, and the Netherlands.

reinterpret, the injunction set out in *Manusmriti* against crossing the black waters.

Although this does not counter the claim that Hinduism is best described as an ethnic religion—as most migrant Hindus have retained the practice of caste marriage and have not sought to widen the definition of who is a Hindu—it does invite scholars to review ideas about where and how Hinduism may be practised. The foundation of temples and the migration of brahmins able to carry out life-cycle rites, fire rituals (*yajna*), and *puja* have allowed Hindus to establish sacred spaces and perform the necessary religious activities outside India. Does this mean that the sacred territory of *bharat* has been extended, as we saw in the cases of Madho Singh and the early Brahmin migrants to south-east Asia? What of those religious organizations, in many countries, which have been founded, managed, and led by enthusiastic and skilful lay persons who have raised funds, purchased property, organized festivals, youth and women's groups, the visits of spiritual leaders, and the employment of brahmins? Although lay people have generally facilitated rather than led public religious activities, they have stepped in when needed to conduct worship and serve the deities directly. The commitment to divine well-being has been considered more important than orthodox brahminical regulation. As Chapters 5 and 7 show, the *bhakti* tradition within Hinduism offers the precedent and context for this.

In countries outside India, temples (*mandir*) have often been fashioned from converted premises, from schools, deconsecrated

10. Greetings from the Shri Swaminarayan Hindu Mandir, London.

churches, homes, even factories. As Hindu communities have grown wealthier, however, they have opened purpose-built temples, designed either according to local styles or in imitation of those in India. In August 1995, the local population of the north London suburb of Neasden, with many thousands of Hindu devotees and invited guests, saw the opening of what *Reader's Digest* magazine described as the 'Eighth Wonder of the World', 'London's answer to the Taj Mahal'. Built from natural materials to Hindu scriptural specifications, and erected entirely by voluntary labour, the Shri Swaminarayan Mandir was the first traditional North Indian style Hindu temple to be built in Europe (see Figure 10). Since its opening it has been used for the regular worship and meetings of the Swaminarayan Hindu Mission, a Gujarati Hindu movement or *sampradaya* headed by a popular Indian guru, Pramukh Swami Maharaj.

The temple is at least as important, however, as a tourist site. Approached through rows of ordinary terraced housing and set back from one of London's busiest roads, it represents Hinduism in all its grandeur to non-Hindus, and shows what can be achieved by devotional service to God. As well as a tour round the magnificent temple with its marble, limestone, and teak carvings, visitors can expect to see a film showing its construction and an exhibition of Hindu heritage. On the opposite side of the road is the Swaminarayan School, one of only a small number of Hindu day schools in the UK.

The Bochasanwasi Akshar Purushottam Sanstha, of which the Swaminarayan Hindu Mission is the British branch, is one of the fastest-growing religious movements among Gujarati Hindus world-wide. With a network of more than 800 temples, 3,300 centres, and hundreds of thousands of followers globally, it has held important cultural festivals in East Africa, Britain, and the USA, as well as in India. It is a devotional movement in the theological tradition of Ramanuja, in which followers worship Swaminarayan as their supreme Lord. It provides single-sex educational and spiritual programmes for children, young people, and those in older age groups. It holds mass rallies and engages actively in voluntary work in all the countries in which it has a presence. It is just one of a number of popular *sampradayas* or sectarian groups operating within the Hindu diaspora.

Some *sampradayas* remain almost exclusively 'Indian', though their membership includes those who are second-, third-, even fourth-generation Indian Americans, Indo-Caribbeans, British Indians, and African Indians. However, other global Hindu movements have a mixed membership, consisting of Indian Hindus *and* those from other ethnic and religious backgrounds. They offer a spiritual message and Hindu ideas and practices to those who were not born or nurtured as Hindus. The Vedanta Society, for example, first started by Vivekananda in America, now has both Indian and non-Indian members. The Hare Krishna movement or ISKCON, the Shaiva Siddhanta Church, the Sai Baba Fellowship, and Shri Mata Amritanandamayi Devi's Amma movement have similar broad appeal, but there are others whose following has been drawn largely from among westerners. These include the American Self-Realization Fellowship founded by Yogananda Paramahamsa, Transcendental Meditation (which excited the interest of the Beatles in the late 1960s), Swami Muktananda's Siddha Yoga, the Neo-Sannyas programme of Bhagwan Rajneesh (also known as Osho), Mataji Nirmala Devi's Sahaja Yoga, and Iyengar Yoga. All of these, together with the mixed membership groups, acknowledge the interest of westerners in aspects of Hindu spirituality, especially in the chanting of *mantras, kundalini* meditation, *hatha yoga*, belief in reincarnation, and vegetarianism. Their timely presence in the West has helped to fill a spiritual vacuum and to offer ideas and practices to those seeking alternatives to western religions and secularism.

This trend has sparked debate among Hindus about the nature of Hinduism and its boundaries. Are movements which offer only selected aspects of Hindu spirituality, like yoga, and make no reference to the Hindu social world authentically Hindu? Have Hindu ideas and practices been transformed beyond recognition in the process? Are members of such groups 'Hindus', or can a Hindu identity only be claimed by one born into an Indian or Indian-diaspora family? I address these questions in Chapter 9.

The role of the guru has been important in most of these contemporary movements, regardless of their membership. Gurus have been a focus for devotion, the mediators of tradition in the alien environment of the West, and the source of authority for those seeking knowledge or guidance. Some have offered systems of spiritual discipline requiring considerable effort and commitment; others, the repetition of a simple *mantra* or a short act of worship as the focus for happiness or self-realization. Some gurus have been controversial and colourful characters, while others have been quietly charismatic. All have shown an astute awareness of the special demands posed by the western context.

Gurus have not been the only individuals to have a special role in the reproduction of Hinduism outside India, however. Within the Indian Hindu diaspora, family members, particularly women, have been vital in communicating Hinduism to the next generation. Temples have established classes to teach community languages, and *sampradayas* have formed youth groups to enhance children's knowledge of scripture and doctrine, but it is in the home that children still learn their first religious lessons. There they are told stories about the gods and goddesses by their elders, read them in comic books, or watch them on tablets or smart phones. They learn about Hindu festivals such as *Divali*, *Mahashivaratri*, *Durga Puja*, *Pongal*, and *Janamashtami*, getting to know the family customs associated with each. Like young children in India, they also learn, by participation and imitation, how to perform *puja* at the home shrine and how to keep fasts. Like Madhur Jaffrey (see Chapter 4), some of them play-act Hindu stories or rituals, and young girls in particular may have real roles to perform as handmaidens of the Goddess in ceremonies associated with her worship. However, these children may not have the same experiences as those in India of having Hindu ethical, social, and cultural traditions present in the world around them as, in most of the countries to which they have migrated, Hindus live as minorities. In many countries their religion has been tolerated but given little if any recognition in the media or state education; in others, multicultural and integration policies have operated giving Hindus an opportunity along with other religious communities to have their voices heard and their religion represented.

A tension arises in the Hindu diaspora, as indeed it does in India, between two important requirements. One is the need to create a strong, unified Hindu identity which can be articulated publicly and presented on a par with other major world religions. The other is the desire of many to stress the openness of Hinduism towards other religions and the diversity of paths within it. The Vishwa Hindu Parishad supports the first of these positions and is active around the world in promoting *Hindutva* or 'Hindu-ness' and a sense of pride among Hindus. A number of Hindu scholars, writers, and women's groups outside India have put forward the opposing view, of religious and cultural multiplicity and difference, arguing that the idea of Hindu unity is both ahistorical and unhelpful in enabling Hindus to live positively with people of other religions and even with those in their own faith community who have differing perspectives.

There is no single version of Hinduism operating among Hindus in diaspora. Hindus of many castes and sects and from many parts of India have migrated, taking with them traditions that were familiar to them back home. They have also been influenced in the reproduction of their religious practices and beliefs by the place in which they settled and its particular social and religious character. However, while developing their own local communities, they have remained in touch with Hindus world-wide, through kin, caste, and sectarian links via Facebook, Skype, email, and mobile phones, and through news, entertainment, and religious websites. These national and global networks have been instrumental in keeping Hindus informed and connected, and for transmitting ideas and opinions.

Hinduism Today is an online and print newspaper for Hindus around the world. It is marketed by its publisher, the Himalayan Academy, as 'The Hindu Family Newspaper Affirming the Dharma and Recording the Modern History of Nearly a Billion Members of a Global Religion in Renaissance'. It features articles on Hindu concepts, practices, traditions, and figures, and stories about Hindus in different countries. It also carries advertisements and notices of relevance to local Hindus. In the Spring 2015 issue, for example, there were stories about cow protection, the Nanda Devi Raj pilgrimage, the Hindu World Congress, a Balinese Hindu festival in Germany, sacred dance, and Hindu schooling. There were letters and book reviews, and an article from the 'publisher's desk' on Hindu views of God.

As *Hinduism Today* shows, in and beyond India Hinduism is subject to continuity and change. New concerns arise, such as ethical issues surrounding reproduction and genetics, and new contexts demand a fresh approach. The presence of Hinduism as a religion alongside others requires Hindus to think about and articulate what is important to them in ways which can be understood by outsiders. Yet the challenge of passing down what is sacred to new generations of insiders remains ever-pressing, as the words of this first-generation British Hindu woman show:

> Well, my parents were born and brought up in India so their life was different. I have many roles to fulfil, not just as a mother, but as a working wife, while my mother and grandmother only had one life, that of a housewife bringing up the family. I have tried my best to transmit my own culture and religion to my children because in this country they couldn't get this religious experience or culture in the outside world. My mother and grandmother didn't have to face this because at home [in India] children picked up religion. You were born and brought up with it. It was everywhere. My children were born in one environment, but they were facing a very different one outside the home. I'm not sure if I've been successful, but I think I've done my best.

Chapter 9
Hindu *dharma*, Hinduism, and hinduisms

What do you see when you look at the image in Figure 11? A cow? But what does that mean to you? A farm animal (in this case, out of place in a city street), a source of meat and milk, leather, and manure? But an Indian viewer, while noting this ordinary cow, might go beyond it to see a sacred symbol, divine mother of all, in whose dung the goddess of prosperity resides. What you see depends on your standpoint.

11. A Mumbai street scene.

A cow signifies something different to Hindus and non-Hindus; but even within Hinduism her meaning differs depending on whether you are a brahmin or a leather worker, one who milks her or uses her products for fuel and cooking.

Hinduism is a bit like this, too. Outsiders and insiders see Hinduism differently, and those who are inside don't always think alike, as we have seen in previous chapters. It would be convenient to offer a simple definition of Hinduism or to categorize it neatly, but it refuses such treatment. To say a cow is an animal or Hinduism a religion tells us very little indeed. What type of animal? What type of religion? And what about the symbolic significance of cows among Hindus?

Defining Hinduism

To call Hinduism a religion raises the question, 'What is a religion?' The term 'religion' is western in origin. It comes from Latin and originally meant the bond between people and their gods. In the study of religions, the principal example has been Christianity. By extension, 'other religions' have been those systems which have been judged to be analogous to Christianity, principally Judaism and Islam, both of which are western and related historically to Christianity, but also eastern systems such as Buddhism and Hinduism. Some of the key characteristics of Christianity against which 'other' religions have been compared and contrasted have been belief in a transcendent God, a founder, scripture, priests, an institution or church, and various dimensions such as belief, ethics, myth, and ritual.

Hinduism, like Christianity, does indeed have a God: one ultimate reality and many gods and goddesses, in fact. But it has no founder, a multitude of scriptures rather than one book, brahmins but no priests in the Christian sense, and no central institution like a church. Ritual, myth, and ethics are important, but belief is of less significance, there being no core creed and few common teachings. But there might also be things intrinsic to Hinduism that just don't show up in a comparison with Christianity. For example, Hinduism extends into the complex socio-religious system of caste and the varied popular practices which, in Christian terms, constitute magic and superstition rather than religion. So, if Hinduism is a religion at all, it is a rather different one to Christianity, if the latter is to be the benchmark for religion. Readers may look for books on Hinduism in the 'Religion' section of libraries and bookshops, but they would be advised to try a few other sections as well.

One modern Hindu philosopher, Sarvepalli Radhakrishnan, declared Hinduism to be 'a way of life'. By doing so, he made the point that it was not something separate from society and politics, from making money, sex, and love, and getting an education. And, like other modern Hindus, he suggested that the closest term to be found within Indian thought and practice was Hindu *dharma*, the law, order, truth, and duties of the Hindu people.

This raises other questions. Whose *dharma* was intended? What does the term 'Hindu' mean? Unlike the term 'Hinduism', which was used first in the early 19th century by orientalist scholars to signify the religion of the 'Hindoos', the term 'Hindu' was of earlier derivation. It had been used by incomers to India, particularly Persians and Turks, to denote those people living around the river Indus in the north and, later on, all the people beyond the Indus, the entire population of India. By that token, Buddhists and Jains, Dravidians and Aryans were all included. The term when used by incomers had no obvious religious significance, referring only to a geographically defined group containing immense internal diversity of language and custom. Later, indigenous Indians began to use the term, too, though only in order to distinguish themselves from the Mughals and Europeans. Still it had no religious connotation, rather an ethnic or national meaning.

But the meaning of 'Hindu' began to change. With the discovery by the British of Vedic scriptures and the brahmin class and culture, it began to be invested with religious significance (on the principal of it being analogous to the term 'Christian'). 'Hindoo' and, later, 'Hinduism' began to be identified with the religious traditions of the Aryan people, and this identification began also to be made by Indian reformers, though the idea of peoplehood and nation continued to be important in the light of calls for Indian self-rule.

Among scholars of religion the meaning and validity of 'Hinduism' has been much discussed as knowledge of its origins has grown. But more than anything, it is awareness of the internal complexity of 'Hinduism' which has called the term into question. Not only does it comprise the major divisions of Vaishnavism, Shaivism, and Shaktism, but it also offers a variety of different philosophical approaches, thousands of deities and their associated mythology and iconography, and innumerable ritual practices. It contains within it brahminism, which is often referred to as the orthodox or mainstream movement within Hinduism, as well as 'Hindu' challenges to brahminism, like those examined in Chapter 7. And then there are the village traditions which extend beyond brahminism to pragmatic, magical, and animist practices. Nowadays, when scholars refer to 'Hinduism', they include all of these movements, traditions, beliefs, and practices. This explains the attraction of the other term mentioned in this chapter's title, 'hinduisms'. There do indeed seem to be many hinduisms rather than one Hinduism. But this invites further questions. Are they not related? If they are, how are they linked?

The question of the relationship between the various religious movements and traditions, beliefs, and practices in India is difficult. Various non-Hindu and Hindu commentators have identified possible connections, particularly the caste system, the authority of the *Veda*, the concept of *dharma*, and Aryan identity. Others have denied the validity of such claims. Looking back over the contents of this book at the interlocking themes, it is possible to see that all those mentioned earlier, plus the popular narrative traditions of the *Ramayana*, reverence for the *Bhagavad-gita*, the presence of the divine in many names and forms, the place of the guru, and the sacred land of India, might also constitute defining features. There seem to be family resemblances between the various parts, but these resemblances are not always the same, just as grandparents, parents, siblings, aunts, uncles, and cousins may not all have the 'family features', but may resemble one another in many different ways, some physical, some in terms of personality or attributes.

Pushing the family metaphor further, like relatives within a family, the various hinduisms exist in tension with one another, some being more alike than others, some being in fierce disagreement with one another. Although Buddhism and Jainism were traditionally seen as heterodox systems and, later, the incoming religions of Islam and Christianity were also seen by Hindus as categorically distinct, this does not mean that all the movements, schools, and traditions within the family of Hinduism were equally accepted by all. There are innumerable accounts of great contests between exponents of different branches of the *vedanta* school, and between those who followed different deities or gurus. And we have seen how rebellious *bhakti* poets and marginal groups criticized and challenged conservative, patriarchal brahmin elders and their social and ritual dominance.

The human metaphors of the family and family resemblance are not just a convenient way of holding together the different hinduisms or related aspects of Hinduism. They also help us to see the importance of power within it. It is all too easy to ignore this factor in thinking about religion, particularly today when spirituality rather than other elements of religion is so often stressed. Many Hindu writers have made this point. As *dharma* or 'a way of life', Hinduism is related to what westerners refer to as 'secular' concerns, to economic, political, and social matters. In India, debates about religious identity are not just about religion, but neither are they just political or social debates in a religious guise. Just as family members try to make their voices heard, even to get the upper hand in day-to-day disputes, so Hindu individuals and groups struggle by whatever means to assert their beliefs and commitments, their caste interests, and sectarian viewpoints. This has included the drive by some Hindu nationalists and political figures to represent 'Hinduism' as a single unified cultural system and 'Hindutva' as a shared religious identity.

A dynamic symbol: the cow and Hinduism

This brings me to the final stage in this investigation of Hinduism—an assessment of what it has meant for modern Hindus and how they have used the term. The cow is my assistant in this, as her destiny as a symbol has been similar to that of Hinduism itself.

Even before the modern period, the cow was associated with several ideas: *ahimsa* or non-injury; purity and purification; goodness; and motherhood, in nurturing and providing not only for her calf but for all. In the Vedic period she was sometimes offered in sacrifice, but later it became an offence to eat her. In the *Mahabharata* and *Manusmriti*, she was associated with Shri, the goddess of prosperity, her products were considered to be pure and good, and she was to be revered as a great mother and provider. Both cows and women were referred to as goddesses, though the cow seems to have had a higher status because of her purity and value as a resource.

In the 19th century, her significance took a new turn. One of the things which distinguished the indigenous Indians or Hindus from incomers was their reverence for the cow and commitment to keeping her from harm. Sacrificing her or eating her, as Muslims and Christians were prone to do, was abhorrent to caste Hindus, and, in the context of a rise in religious self-consciousness among reforming groups, protection of the cow became a symbol for Hindu identity. The cow was identified as mother of the nation. Dayananda Saraswati of the Arya Samaj and Gandhi both wrote about the national importance of protecting the cow, and local societies were established throughout India to engage ordinary Hindus in looking after this great symbol.

The importance given to the cow puzzled those outsiders who knew little about Hinduism. Arguments took place among western scholars about whether the status of the cow in India could be justified on economic grounds. What they failed to appreciate was her symbolic value. She was both religiously *and* economically important. But the cow's place in Hinduism was questioned by insiders, too, as a patriarchal symbol and one with dubious implications for untouchables whose lowly status was reinforced by her representation of purity.

What does this extended illustration reveal about the destiny of Hinduism in the modern period? I have sought to show how the idea of the cow came to have symbolic significance for Hindus in the context of British India, becoming a focus for religious, political, and scholarly discussion and negotiation. The idea of 'Hinduism' only came to the fore in the modern period, but, like the symbol of the cow, it had its antecedents in the scriptures, practices, concepts, and institutions of earlier times. The phrase *sanatana dharma*, eternal tradition, used often by Hindus to describe their religion, implies antiquity, but its usage is modern.

The socio-religious traditions of the Hindus have endured for several millennia, and were clearly not an invention of the modern period. However, the particular interpretations given to them by orientalists, reformers, nationalists, the women's movement, and the *dalit* liberationists—to name just a few—have led to the creation of 'Hinduism' and the modern debate about its nature.

So, the cow as a symbol for the nation and Hinduism as a type of religion are modern ideas in India, and both are still evolving. New movements, for example, have changed the face of Hinduism, bringing social reform, animal welfare, and Hindu spirituality to the fore. A moral imperative for the future of Hinduism, according to many Hindus, is its need to transform itself in order to be more open to marginal groups: Arvind Sharma's discussion of *karma* and caste (see Chapter 3) is a response to this. The invitation made by religious nationalists to a *dalit* to lay the foundation stone for the planned temple to Rama in Ayodhya, and the acceptance of women renouncers in some modern movements are further examples. Such trends run counter to traditional teachings, and illustrate that religious change is as much a part of Hinduism as the continuity of tradition (as witnessed in other chapters).

Ideas about the nature of Hinduism are also evolving within the debate about Hindu nationalism. India is formally a secular country, in which Hindus (by which I mean those who are not Muslims, Buddhists, Christians, etc.) are in the majority. Yet, the idea of the sacred land of India, her people and, by extension, the nation, are central to discussions about Hinduism. Claims and counter-claims about the early Indian Aryans and Dravidians, about unity and diversity within Hinduism, and the multi-religious history of India all contribute to the discussion about whether Hinduism can and should be the national religion or whether India should continue to endorse and celebrate its religious plurality. The cow remains a focus of this debate, with the consumption of beef at the heart of the struggle between Hindu nationalists and those who see India first and foremost as a secular state encompassing diverse religious communities with differing cultural practices.

And, finally, what about the idea of Hinduism as a global religion? Although most Hindus continue to live in India, there are Hindu communities everywhere, making Hinduism a world religion. This is supported further by the relatively recent practice of taking the message of Hindu spirituality to non-Hindus. Whether the new movements that have done so are properly 'Hindu' continues to be debated, but the practice has helped the spread of Hindu ideas. The cow has found a place in global Hindu spirituality too. She remains relevant as a symbol of non-violence, but in a new context of environmental awareness, widespread vegetarianism, and a commitment to the integrity of all creation.

'Hinduism' defies people's desire to define and categorize it. It is *both* a dynamic phenomenon of the modern world, evolving from the combined imaginations of many individuals and groups, Hindu and non-Hindu, *and* the sum of its many parts—its traditions, myths, institutions, rituals, and ideas—its many hinduisms. It has the power and diversity to capture the imaginations of Hindus and non-Hindus alike, and the capacity to challenge preconceived ideas about what a religion is.

Like other religions, Hinduism, whilst drawing on the legacy of its philosophical and cultural traditions, is shaped and changed by novel contexts and challenges. Hindus in India and beyond continue to find ways to respond to the new demands arising from ethical issues, technological innovation, migration, social change and exposure to other religions and cultures. Increasingly, they are required to do so in a global context where 'religion' is often pitted against other systems, ideologies, and customary practices, and where it has to be publicly explained and justified.

The challenges encountered by Hindus in a Hindu-majority state will differ from those of minority Hindus but, in a context where all nations are now interconnected and diverse, both groups will be called on to acknowledge and work with non-Hindu others in their midst as well as those who are vulnerable within their own communities. The resources offered by Hinduism's complex and multifaceted traditions may well be drawn on to help cope with such situations and to support those facing change. However, future generations of Hindus will want to practise and identify with Hinduism in their own ways and not simply replicate those of their forebears. Being confident and knowledgeable as Hindus, without being defensive or aggressive, in a situation where religion in general and Hinduism in particular are not well known or understood will itself be a challenge.

Appendix
The six philosophical systems (*darshana*)

The *Vedanta* system is one of six orthodox (*astika*) perspectives or systems (*darshana*) commonly identified in Hindu thought. Each has a *Sutra* text and commentaries which explain and interpret it. The western distinction between philosophy and theology has little relevance for understanding the *darshanas*. They contain logic, analysis, and scriptural exegesis, and are often directed to the liberation or salvation of the self.

1. *Samkhya*: This dualistic and atheistic perspective focuses upon the distinctive nature of *purusha*, self or spirit, and *prakriti*, matter.
2. *Yoga*: The *yoga-darshana* builds on the dualism of *samkhya* but focuses on the spiritual discipline required for the self to attain liberation.
3. *Mimamsa*: Focusing on *dharma*, right action, this is a system of Vedic exegesis.
4. *Vedanta*: Also an exegetical system, *Vedanta* refers to the 'end of the *Veda*', particularly the Upanishadic teaching on ultimate reality (*brahman*).
5. *Nyaya*: A system of logic, leading to liberation.
6. *Vaisheshika*: A system of atomistic analysis of the categories of *dharma* and their constituent elements.

Timeline

Before Christian Era (BCE)

2600–1800	Indus valley period
1500–500	Vedic period; composition of Vedic texts (*Samhitas, Brahmanas, Aranyakas, Upanishads*)
500–100 CE	Composition of *Mahabharata* (including the *Bhagavad-gita*) and Ramayana; composition of *sutras*, including *Manusmriti, Brahma-sutra*
490–400	Approximate dates for life of the Buddha according to recent research
200–200 CE	Buddhism and Jainism widespread in India

Christian Era (CE)

100–500	Migration of Hindus to south-east Asia
300–900	Composition of *Puranas*
400–	Spread of Vaishnavism; beginnings of Tantrism
500–	*Devi-mahatmya* composed; spread of Shaktism; growth of temple cult and use of iconography
500–950	Flourishing of south Indian *bhakti* poetry
600–1000	Brahminical revival; decline of Buddhism in India
700–1100	Development of *Shaiva* theology

788–820	Life of Shankara
1000–	Muslim incursions into north-west India
1017–1137	Life of Ramanuja
1197–1276	Life of Madhva
1211–1526	Delhi Sultanate
*c.*1420	Life of Mirabai
1440–1518	Life of Kabir
*c.*1469	Birth of Guru Nanak, the first of the Sikh gurus
1485–1533	Life of Chaitanya
1498	Portuguese arrival in south India (Vasco da Gama)
1526–1757	Mughal rule in India
1650	British East India Company established in Bengal
1757	Victory of Clive at the Battle of Plassey
1772	Warren Hastings made Governor-General
1772–1833	Life of Ram Mohan Roy
1774	Asiatic Society founded by William Jones
1775	Translation of *Bhagavad-gita* by Charles Wilkins
1813	Missionary activity in India legalized by British Government
1820s	Growth of Swaminarayan movement
1824–83	Life of Dayananda Saraswati
1828	Brahmo Samaj formed
1829	Prohibition of *sati*
1836–86	Life of Ramakrishna
1838	Beginning of indenture system in which Indian labourers were transported to the Caribbean, Fiji, and Mauritius
1858–1922	Life of Pandita Ramabai
1863–1902	Life of Vivekananda

1869–1948	Life of Mohandas Gandhi
1875	Arya Samaj formed; Theosophical Society formed in New York
1879–1926	Life of Sarojini Naidu
1885	Founding of Indian National Congress
1886	Ramakrishna Order formed (Ramakrishna Mission founded in 1897)
1891–1956	Life of Dr B. R. Ambedkar
1893	World Parliament of Religions, Chicago
1894	First Vedanta Society founded in New York
1896–1982	Life of Anandamayi Ma
1917	Women's India Association formed
1930	Salt march, led by Gandhi
1947	Partition of India and Indian independence
1949	Shaiva Siddhanta Church founded; incorporated under United States law in California in 1957
*c.*1950–	Migration of Hindus to West for work
1950	Constitution of India accepted
1953	Birth of Mata Amritanandamayi, founder of Amma
1954	Sarada Devi Math and Mission founded
1955	Untouchability Offences Act
1961	Dowry Prohibition Act
1966	Founding of the International Society for Krishna Consciousness by A. C. Bhaktivedanta Swami
1983	Beginning of Tamil Hindu migration from war torn Sri Lanka to Europe and North America
1990	Scheduled Caste and Scheduled Tribe (Prevention of Atrocities) Act
1992	Destruction of Babri mosque in Ayodhya by Hindu extremists

1995	Opening of first traditional, North Indian style temple in Europe, the Swaminarayan Hindu Mandir, London
1997	K. R. Narayanan, a *dalit*, elected President of India
2014	Five men from scheduled castes and two women installed as priests to serve alongside Brahmins at the Pandharpur temple in Maharastra, India
2014	Narendra Modi, leader of the Hindu nationalist Bharatiya Janata Party (BJP), became Prime Minister of India

Glossary

Many of the scriptures of Hinduism were composed in Sanskrit (though some later ones were written in Tamil, Hindi, and other regional languages) and the words used in this book and listed in this glossary are mostly Sanskrit terms. In Sanskrit there are long and short vowel sounds, several *s*/*sh* sounds and a number of different sounds for *t* and *d* produced by placing the tongue behind the teeth or at the top of the mouth. If you would like to know more about how to pronounce these words, you might look in *Teach Yourself Sanskrit* or in a dictionary of Sanskrit. Throughout this book I have used common English spellings for Sanskrit terms, but here, as well as showing the meaning of the terms that I have used repeatedly, I have shown how they are formally transliterated from the Devanagri alphabet of Sanskrit using diacritical marks.

There are numerous regional languages in India and some of the terms I have used are rendered differently in each. Different names may be used for deities and different terms for ritual practices.

advaita; *advaita*	non-duality; the form of *vedanta* associated with Shankara
Aranyakas; *Āranyakas*	forest treatises; Vedic scriptures, precursors to the *Upanishads*
ashrama; *āśrama*	stage of life
atman; *ātman*	the self or soul
avatara; *avatāra*	incarnation, usually of the god Vishnu
Bhagavad-gita; *Bhagavād-gītā*	the 'song of the Lord'; an important Hindu scripture, part of the *Mahabharata*

bhakti; *bhakti*	loving devotion
brahman; *brahman*	ultimate reality
Brahmanas; *Brāhmaṇas*	Vedic scriptures in which sacrifices are described
brahmin; *brāhman*	the priestly class or *varna*
chandala; *cāndāla*	perjoratively referred to as 'dog-cookers' in *Manusmriti*, a *chandala* is someone who disposes of the dead, and is deemed untouchable
dalit; *dalit*	the preferred name for those denoted as untouchable
darshana; *darśana*	seeing and being seen by the deity; philosophical perspective or system
Devi; *Devī*	the great Goddess
dharma; *dharma*	duty, law, teaching, order, sometimes 'religion'
Divali; *Divālī*	the festival of lights
Dravidian	name attributed to the indigenous people of India
Durga; *Durgā*	a benevolent warrior goddess
dvaita; *dvaita*	duality; form of *vedanta* associated with Madhva
Ganesha; *Gaṇeśa*	the elephant-headed deity; remover of obstacles
ishvara; *īśvara*	Lord; powerful one
jati; *jāti*	caste
jnana; *jñāna*	knowledge
karma; *karma*	action
Krishna; *Kṛṣṇa*	a popular deity, depicted as a baby, cowherder, and charioteer; *avatara* of Vishnu
kshatriya; *kṣatriya*	warrior class or *varna*
linga; *liṅga*	a symbol associated with Shiva
Madhva; *Madhva*	thirteenth-century philosopher
Mahabharata; *Mahābhārata*	a popular epic text and source of many stories about *dharma*
mandir; *maṇḍir*	a temple
mantra; *mantra*	a verbal formula or sound which is full of power
Manusmriti; *Manusmṛti*	(also *Laws of Manu*) a religio-legal text describing duties of different social groups

murti; *mūrti*	an icon of a deity
puja; *pūjā*	worship in which offerings are made to a deity
Purana; *Puṛāṇa*	ancient; mythological and genealogical texts containing stories of gods and goddesses
Radha; *Radhā*	the consort of Krishna
Rama; *Rāma*	a popular deity beloved as king of Ayodhya; an *avatara* of Vishnu
Ramanuja; *Rāmānuja*	an eleventh-century philosopher
Ramayana; *Rāmāyana*	the popular epic telling the story of Rama, Sita, and Lakshmana, of which there are many versions
Rig Veda; *Ṛg Veda*	the earliest Vedic text, containing hymns to the deities
rishi; *ṛṣi*	a sage
sampradaya; *saṃpradāya*	tradition; lineage through which teachings are handed down
samsara; *saṃsāra*	the cycle of birth, death, and re-birth; the world
sannyasa; *saṇnyāsa*	renunciation; the final stage of life; also *sannyasi*, one who has renounced the world
sati; *satī*	a virtuous wife; wife who burns on the funeral pyre of her husband
Shaiva; *Śaiva*	a follower of Shiva
Shakta; *Śākta*	a follower of the Goddess
shakti; *śakti*	divine power or energy personified as female; a name for the Goddess
Shankara; *Śaṇkara*	a ninth-century philosopher
Shankara-acharya; *Śaṇkarācārya*	a spiritual leader of the Order of Shankara
Shiva; *Śiva*	a major deity frequently depicted as an ascetic; auspicious one, also associated with destruction
shruti; *śrūti*	revealed; those early scriptures held to be revealed to *rishis* or sages
shudra; *śūdra*	artisan class or *varna*
Sita; *Sītā*	the consort of Rama, often described as the perfect wife
smriti; *smṛti*	remembered; those scriptures held to be remembered and handed down by tradition
sutra; *sūtra*	thread; an aphoristic text

Upanishad; *Upaniṣad*	sitting near a teacher; secret doctrine; those early scriptures in which sages enquired about the nature of ultimate reality and the self
Vaishnava; *Vaiṣṇava*	a follower of Vishnu
varna; *varna*	social class or estate
varna-ashrama-dharma; *varnāśramadharma*	duties according to one's social position and stage of life
Veda; *Veda*	knowledge; earliest Hindu scriptures, associated with the Aryans
vedanta; *vedānta*	the 'end of the *Veda*'; a philosophical system exploring the nature of *brahman*
vishishta; *viśiṣṭa*	qualified non-duality; the form of *vedanta* associated with Ramanuja
Vishnu; *Viṣṇu*	one who pervades everything; a major deity who maintains all; source of *avataras*
yajna; *yajña*	sacrifice; Vedic ritual practice in which offerings were made to the deities, often in a fire
yoga; *yoga*	yoking; focusing or concentrating; discipline; a system for attaining liberation

References

Chapter 1: The scholar and the devotee

Nirad Chaudhuri, *Hinduism: A Religion to Live By* (Oxford: Oxford University Press, 1979), 311–29.

Chapter 2: Revelation and the transmission of knowledge

R. K. Narayan, *Gods, Demons and Others* (London: Mandarin, 1990), 2–4; *Rig Veda* 1.1 in Wendy Doniger O'Flaherty, *Textual Sources for the Study of Hinduism* (Chicago: University of Chicago Press, 1990), 10; *Manusmriti* 2.11 in Wendy Doniger O'Flaherty (ed.), *The Laws of Manu* [*The Laws of Manu* is another name for the *Manusmriti*] (Harmondsworth: Penguin, 1991); Brian K. Smith, *Reflections on Resemblance, Ritual, and Religion* (New York and Oxford: Oxford University Press, 1989), 13–17; *Rig Veda* 10.90 in Ainslee T. Embree, *Sources of Indian Tradition*, vol. i, 2nd edn (New York: Columbia University Press, 1988), 17–19; R. K. Narayan, *The Guide* (London: Mandarin, 1990).

Chapter 3: Understanding the self

Hinduism Today, http://www.hinduismtoday.com/ (see Archive for November 1994 edition); 'Meeting Amma', *Amma*, http://www.amritapuri.org/amma/who/darshan; *Upanisads* (tr. Patrick Olivelle, Oxford: Oxford University Press, 1996), 154–5; *The Complete Works of Vivekananda*, vol. viii (Calcutta: Advaita Ashrama, 1970), 101; *The Bhagavad Gita* 2.24 (tr. W. J. Johnson, Oxford: Oxford University

Press, 1994), 9; *The Bhagavad Gita* 3.4, Johnson, 15; *The Bhagavad Gita* on practice of *yogin*: Johnson, 28; Patanjali on *yoga sutra*: Vivian Worthington, *A History of Yoga* (London: Arkana, 1989), 69–78; Bal Gangadhar Tilak, *Gita Rahasya* (Poona, 1935); Mahatma Gandhi on *karma yoga*: Mahadev Desai, *The Gita According to Gandhi* (Ahmedabad: Navajivan, 1946); Arvind Sharma, *Hinduism for Our Times* (Oxford and Delhi: Oxford University Press, 1996), 36–46; *The Bhagavad Gita*, Johnson, 7–13; Sharma, *Hinduism for Our Times*, 42.

Chapter 4: Divine heroes: the epic tradition

Madhur Jaffrey, *Seasons of Splendour: Tales, Myths and Legends of India* (London: Pavilion Books, 1985), 8; Debjani Chatterjee, *I was that Woman* (Frome: Hippopotamus Press, 1989), 23–4.

Chapter 5: The divine presence

Pierre Martin in P. J. Marshall, *The British Discovery of Hinduism in the Eighteenth Century* (Cambridge: Cambridge University Press, 1970), 21; Henry Martyn in George Smith, *The Life of Henry Martin* (London, 1892), 163; *Upanisads*, Olivelle, 46.

Chapter 6: Hinduism, colonialism, and modernity

Kabir, 'Warnings' (tr. Daniel Gold), in Wendy Doniger O'Flaherty, *Textual Sources for the Study of Hinduism* (Chicago: University of Chicago Press, 1990), 140–1; Kabir, 'The World is Mad' (tr. Linda Hess and Sukdev Singh), in Ainslee T. Embree, *Sources of Indian Tradition*, vol. i, 2nd edn (New York: Columbia University Press, 1988), 375; Warren Hastings in P. J. Marshall, *The British Discovery of Hinduism in the Eighteenth Century* (Cambridge: Cambridge University Press, 1970), 189; Abbé Dubois, *Hindu Manners, Customs, and Ceremonies*, 3rd edn (Oxford: Clarendon Press, 1906), 8; Walt Whitman, *Leaves of Grass* (Oxford: Oxford University Press, 1990); Agehananda Bharati, 'The Hindu Renaissance and its Apologetic Patterns', *Journal of Asian Studies* (29, 1970), 273; Rajiv Malhotra, *Indra's Net: Defending Hinduism's Philosophical Unity* (Delhi: HarperCollins, 2014).

Chapter 7: Challenges to Hinduism: women and *dalits*

Chandalas as 'dog-cookers' in Wendy Doniger O'Flaherty (ed.), *The Laws of Manu* (Harmondsworth: Penguin, 1991) 10.108; high caste women in O'Flaherty, *The Laws of Manu* 5.146–69; Sarojini Naidu in Manohar Kaur, *Role of Women in the Freedom Movement, 1857–1947* (Delhi: Sterling, 1968), 111; women's prayer in Laxmi G. Tiwari, *A Splendour of Worship: Women's Fasts, Rituals, Stories and Art* (Delhi: Manohar, 1991), 8; *India at a Glance: Population Census 2011—Final* (http://www.census2011.co.in/sexratio.php); 'Crime Against SC/ST', *IndiaStat* (http://www.indiastat.com/crimeandlaw/6/incidenceofcrime/130/crimeagainstscst/17913/stats.aspx); B. K. Ambedkar (tr. Vasant W. Moon) in Barbara R. Joshi (ed.), *Untouchable: Voices of the Dalit Liberation Movement* (London: Zed Books, 1986), 30–1; Neerav Patel, 'Burning at Both the Ends', in Joshi, *Untouchable*, 42.

Chapter 8: Crossing the black waters: Hinduism beyond India

Richard Burghart (ed.), *Hinduism in Great Britain: The Perpetuation of Religion in an Alien Cultural Milieu* (London: Tavistock, 1987), 1–2; Steven Vertovec, *Hindu Trinidad: Religion, Ethnicity and Socio-economic Change* (London: Macmillan Caribbean, 1992); 'Hinduism by Country', *Wikipedia: The Free Encyclopedia*, http://en.wikipedia.org/wiki/Hinduism_by_country (including in-country statistics and figures from the Pew Research Center and the US State Department); April/May/June 2015 issue, *Hinduism Today*, http://hinduismtoday.com/; quotation from an interview by Kim Knott with 'Priya', a British Hindu woman.

Chapter 9: Hindu *dharma*, Hinduism, and hinduisms

Sarvepalli Radhakrishnan, *The Hindu View of Life* (London: Mandala, 1988), 55.

Further reading

Chapter 1: The scholar and the devotee

An excellent resource for the study of Hinduism is the six-volume *Brill's Encyclopedia of Hinduism*. Useful articles include 'Hinduism' by Alf Hiltebeitel in the *Encyclopedia of Religion*, 2nd edn (ed. Lindsay Jones, London and New York: Macmillan, 2005), vol. vi, 3988–4009, and 'Hinduism' by Simon Weightman in *The New Penguin Handbook of the World's Living Religions* (ed. John Hinnells, London: Penguin, 2010). An academic journal with a focus on Hinduism is the *International Journal of Hindu Studies*.

Selected introductory books by Hindu insiders: Nirad Chaudhuri, *Hinduism: A Religion to Live By* (Oxford: Oxford University Press, 1979); Anantanand Rambachan, *The Hindu Vision* (Delhi: Motilal Banarsidass, 1992); Arvind Sharma, *Hinduism for Our Times* (Oxford and Delhi: Oxford University Press, 1996).

Selected introductory books by non-Hindu outsiders: Klaus Klostermaier, *A Survey of Hinduism* (New York: State University of New York Press, 1989); Gavin Flood, *An Introduction to Hinduism* (Cambridge: Cambridge University Press, 1996); Nancy Auer Falk, *Living Hinduisms: An Explorer's Guide* (Belmont, CA: Wadsworth, 2006); Wendy Doniger, *The Hindus: An Alternative History* (Oxford and New York: Oxford University Press, 2010).

Selected books on early India: Romila Thapar, *Early India: From the Origins to AD 1300* (Berkeley: University of California Press, 2004);

Jane Macintosh, *The Ancient Indus Valley: New Perspectives* (Santa Barbara: ABC CLIO inc, 2008); Edwin F. Bryant and Laurie L. Patton (eds.), *The Indo-Aryan Controversy: Evidence and Inference in Indian History* (Abingdon and New York: Routledge, 2005).

Chapter 2: Revelation and the transmission of knowledge

Novels and stories by Hindus are invaluable as a source of information about Hinduism and Hindu society. In addition to *Gods, Demons and Others* and *The Guide* by R. K. Narayan, there are many others by authors including Mulk Raj Anand, Kamala Markandaya, U. R. Anantha Murthy, Anita Desai, and Gita Mehta.

Books on gurus, tradition, and transmission: K. Sivaraman (ed.), *Hindu Spirituality: Vedas Through Vedanta* (New York: Crossroad, 1989)—this is also useful for Chapter 3; Kirin Narayan, *Storytellers, Saints and Scoundrels: Folk Narrative in Hindu Religious Teaching* (Philadelphia: Pennsylvania University Press, 1989); Karen Pechilis (ed.), *The Graceful Guru: Hindu Female Gurus in India and the United States* (Oxford and New York: Oxford University Press, 2004); Jacob Copeman and Aya Ikegame (eds), *The Guru in South Asia: New Interdisciplinary Perspectives* (London and New York: Routledge, 2012).

Chapter 3: Understanding the self

Introductions to Hindu philosophy: Edeltraud Harzer Clear, 'Hindu Philosophy', in E. Craig (ed.), *Routledge Encyclopedia of Philosophy* (London: Routledge, 1998), http://www.rep.routledge.com/article/F002; Andrew J. Nicholson, *Unifying Hinduism: Philosophy and Identity in Indian Intellectual History* (New York and Chichester: University of Columbia Press, 2010); Christopher Bartley, *An Introduction to Indian Philosophy* (London and New York: Continuum, 2011).

Translations of Hindu scriptures: Wendy Doniger O'Flaherty (ed.), *Textual Sources for the Study of Hinduism* (Manchester: Manchester University Press, 1988); Ainslee T. Embree (ed.), *Sources of Indian Tradition*, vol. i, 2nd edn (New York: Columbia University Press, 1988). Selected verses by Shankara, Ramanuja, and Madhva: Sarvepalli Radhakrishnan and Charles A. Moore (eds), *A Sourcebook in Indian Philosophy* (Princeton: Princeton University Press, 1967).

For *karma* and *yoga*, see Sharma, *Hinduism for Our Times*, Rambachan, *The Hindu Vision*, Flood, *An Introduction to Hinduism*, and Klostermaier, *A Survey of Hinduism*.

Websites for Hindu movements: BAPS Swaminarayan Sanstha, http://www.baps.org/; Shri Mata Amritanandamayi Devi movement (Amma), http://www.amritapuri.org/; International Society for Krishna Consciousness, http://iskcon.org/; Shaiva Siddhanta Church, http://www.himalayanacademy.com/. All accessed 15 March 2015.

On religion and new media: Heidi Campbell, *When Religion Meets New Media* (London and New York: Routledge, 2008).

Chapter 4: Divine heroes: the epic tradition

All the episodes of Ramanand Sagar's *Ramayan* can be viewed online at YouTube, https://www.youtube.com. Nina Paley (Dir.), *Sita Sings the Blues* (2008), http://www.sitasingstheblues.com/watch.html. Accessed 15 March 2015.

Retellings in English of stories of the gods and goddesses: Amar Chitra Katha, *Rama, Tales of the Mother Goddess, Mahabharata* (all India Book House); C. Rajagopalachari, *Ramayana* (Bombay: Bharatiya Vidya Bhavan, 1962); Wendy Doniger O'Flaherty, *Hindu Myths* (Harmondsworth: Penguin, 1975); Serinity Young (ed.), *An Anthology of Sacred Texts by and about Women* (London: Pandora, 1993); Paula Richman (ed.), *Ramayana Stories in Modern South Asia: An Anthology*, (Bloomington: Indiana Press University, 2008).

Rama, Sita, and the Devi in Contemporary Hinduism: Paula Richman (ed.), *Many Ramayanas: The Diversity of a Narrative Tradition in South Asia* (Berkeley: University of California Press, 1991); Paula Richman (ed.), *Questioning Ramayanas: A South Asian Tradition* (Berkeley: University of California Press, 2001); John Stratton Hawley and Donna Marie Wulff (eds), *Devi: Goddesses of India* (Berkeley: University of California Press, 1996); Jacqueline Suthren Hurst, *Sita's Story* (Norwich: Chansitor, 1997).

On the place of the *Ramayana* in Hindu nationalism: Peter van der Veer, *Religious Nationalism: Hindus and Muslims in India* (Berkeley: University of California Press, 1994). Omar Rashid, 'Modi Invokes Ram,

EC Seeks Report', *The Hindu* (26 May 2014), http://www.thehindu.com/elections/loksabha2014/modi-invokes-ram-ec-seeks-report/article5978885.ece. Accessed 15 March 2015.

Chapter 5: The divine presence

Most general books, such as those by Rambachan *The Hindu Vision*, Flood, *An Introduction to Hinduism*, and Klostermaier, *A Survey of Hinduism*, contain accounts of Hindu worship, including *puja*, pilgrimage and festivals. See also Christopher J. Fuller, *The Camphor Flame: Popular Hinduism and Society in India* (Princeton: Princeton University Press, 1992).

On Hindu iconography and architecture: Diana Eck, *Darsan: Seeing the Divine Image in India* (Chambersburg, PA: Anima, 1981); George Michell, *The Hindu Temple: An Introduction to its Meaning and Forms* (Chicago and London: Chicago University Press, 1988); Vinayak Bharne and Krupali Krusche, *Rediscovering the Hindu Temple: The Sacred Architecture and Urbanism of India* (Newcastle-Upon-Tyne: Cambridge Scholars Press, 2012).

On worship in Madurai and ISKCON: C. J. Fuller, *The Renewal of the Priesthood: Modernity and Traditionalism in a South Indian Temple* (Princeton: Princeton University Press, 2014; Graham Dwyer and Richard J. Cole (eds.), *The Hare Krishna Movement: Forty Years of Chant and Change* (London and New York: I. B. Tauris, 2007).

Chapter 6: Hinduism, colonialism, and modernity

Examples of *bhakti* poetry in Embree (*Sources of Indian Tradition*) and O'Flaherty (*Textual Sources for the Study of Hinduism*). The lectures and writings of Hindu reformers are quoted extensively in Glyn Richards, *A Sourcebook of Modern Hinduism* (London: Taylor and Francis, 1996).

For Orientalism: P. J. Marshall, *The British Discovery of Hinduism in the Eighteenth Century* (Cambridge: Cambridge University Press, 1970); Carl T. Jackson, *The Oriental Religions and American Thought: Nineteenth-Century Explorations* (Westport, CT: Greenwood Press, 1971); Richard King, *Orientalism and Religion* (Abingdon and New York: Routledge, 1999). On *sati*: J. S. Hawley (ed.), *Sati, the Blessing and the Curse: The Burning of Wives in India* (New York and Oxford: Oxford University Press, 1994).

For the history of the period: Barbara Metcalf and Thomas R. Metcalf, *A Concise History of Modern India* (Cambridge: Cambridge University Press, 2006); for religious movements and personalities, Flood, *An Introduction to Hinduism*. On Gandhi: Bhikhu Parekh, *Gandhi: A Very Short Introduction* (Oxford: Oxford University Press, 2001).

Chapter 7: Challenges to Hinduism: women and *dalits*

On women: Madhu Kishwar and Ruth Vanita (eds.), *In Search of Answers: Indian Women's Voices from Manushi* (London: Zed Books, 1984, repr. New Delhi: Horizon India Books, 1991); Radha Kumar, *The History of Doing: An Illustrated Account of Movements for Women's Rights and Feminism in India, 1800–1990* (New Delhi: Kali for Women, 1993); Tamsin Bradley, Emma Tomalin, and Mangala Subramaniam (eds), *Dowry: Bridging the Gap between Theory and Practice* (New Delhi: Women Unlimited, 2009); Tracy Pintchman (ed.), *Women's Lives, Women's Rituals in the Hindu Tradition* (Oxford and New York: Oxford University Press, 2007); Susie Tharu and K. Lalita (eds), *Women Writing in India, 600 BC to the Early Twentieth Century* (London: Pandora Press, 1991).

On *dalits*: Barbara R. Joshi (ed.), *Untouchable: Voices of the Dalit Liberation Movement* (London: Zed Books, 1984); S. M. Michael (ed.), *Untouchable: Dalits in Modern India* (Boulder and London: Lynne Reiner, 1999); Human Rights Watch, *Hidden Apartheid: Caste Discrimination against India's 'Untouchables'* (NYU School of Law: Center for Human Rights and Global Justice, 2007).

IndiaStat (Crime and Law), http://www.indiastat.com/crimeandlaw/6/incidenceofcrime/130/crimeagainstscst/17913/stats.aspx.

Chapter 8: Crossing the black waters: Hinduism beyond India

Selected books on Hindus and Hinduism beyond India: Robert Jackson and Eleanor Nesbitt, *Hindu Children in Britain* (Stoke-on-Trent: Trentham Books, 1993); Raymond Brady Williams (ed.), *A Sacred Thread: Modern Transmission of Hindu Traditions in India and Abroad* (Chambersburg, PA: Anima, 1992); Joanne Punzo

Waghorne, *Diaspora of the Gods: Modern Hindu Temples in an Urban Middle-Class World* (New York: Oxford University Press, 2004); Prema Kurien, *A Place at the Table: Multiculturalism and the Development of an American Hinduism* (New Brunswick: Rutgers University Press, 2007); John Zavos, Pralay Kanungo, Deepa S. Reddy, Maya Warrier, and Raymond Brady Williams (eds), *Public Hinduisms* (New Delhi: Sage, 2012).

Chapter 9: Hindu *dharma*, Hinduism, and hinduisms

Hinduism and hinduisms, meaning, definition, invention: The general books and articles referred to for Chapter 1 all contain discussions of the meaning of 'Hinduism'. G. D. Sontheimer and H. Kulke (eds), *Hinduism Reconsidered* (Delhi: Manohar, 1991); Sharada Sugirtharaja, *Imagining Hinduism: A Postcolonial Perspective* (London: Routledge, 2003); William Gould, *Hindu Nationalism and the Language of Politics in Late Colonial India* (Cambridge: Cambridge University Press, 2004); Brian Pennington, *Was Hinduism Invented? Britons, Indians and the Colonial Construction of Hinduism* (New York: Oxford University Press, 2005).

Publisher's acknowledgements

We are grateful for permission to include the following copyright material in this book.

Extract from 'Burning at Both the Ends', by Neerav Patel, in Barbara Joshi (ed.), *Untouchable! Voices of the Dalit Liberation Movement* (London: Zed Books, 1986), 42.

Extract from Rig Veda 1.1 (tr O'Flaherty), in Wendy Doniger O'Flaherty (Ed.), *Textual Sources for the Study of Hinduism*, (Manchester University Press, 1988), 6.

Extract from the beginning and end of 'Warnings: couplet 2' by Kabir (tr. Daniel Gold), in Wendy Doniger O'Flaherty (Ed.), *Textual Sources for the Study of Hinduism*, (Manchester University Press, 1988), 140–141.

The publisher and author have made every effort to trace and contact all copyright holders before publication. If notified, the publisher will be pleased to rectify any errors or omissions at the earliest opportunity.

Index

Page numbers in italics refer to pictures or maps

A

advaita vedanta 27, 28, 31, 67, 69, 117
Akkamahadevi 76
Ambedkar, B. K. 81–2, 84, 90, 115
Amma 24, 97, 115
Anandamayi Ma 20–2, 115
Antal 76
Aranyakas 13
Arnold, Sir Edwin 71
Arya Samaj 6, 67–8, 107, 120
Aryans 3–5, 18, 67–8, 104, 105, 109
ashrama 17, 18, 42, 117
Atharva Veda 13, 79
atman 25, 28, 30, 53, 117
  see also self
avatara 43, 50–1, 52, 117
Ayodhya 40–3, 46, 109, 115, 119

B

Besant, Annie 70, 78
Bhagavata Purana 10, 13, 58, 61
Bhagavad-gita 7, 8, 13, 14, 26, 32, 51–3, 71, 106, 113, 114, 121–2
  and *karma* 34–7
  Western commentators on 7, 64
bhakti 51, 76, 84, 95, 118
bhakti poets 14–15, 62, 76, 84–5, 106, 113, 128
bhakti yoga 34, 61
Bhaktivedanta Swami, A. C. 60–1, 115
Bharata 40
Blavatsky, Madame Helena 70
  Western commentators on 70
Brahma Kumaris 85
brahman 15–16, 21, 25, 26, 70, 111
  Madhva on 31
  Ramanuja on 29–30
  Shankara on 21, 28
Brahmanas 13, 15–16
Brahma-sutra 25–6, 67, 113
brahmin 8, 11, 12, 15–19, 20, 26, 42, 49, 60, 66, 68, 75, 78, 85, 87, 88, 91, 92, 95, 103, 104, 106, 116, 118
brahminism 15–19, 28, 29, 35, 46, 65, 74, 83, 84, 85, 91, 95, 105, 113
Brahmo Samaj 8, 67, 69, 114
Brihadaranyaka Upanishad 13, 55
Britain 67, 90, 93, 97
British 3, 4, 6, 16, 44, 63–8, 70–3, 78, 81

Buddha 32, 52, 71, 113
Buddhism 1, 4, 28–9, 82, 84, 103, 106, 113
Burghart, Richard 90–1
Burma 89, 91

C

Cambodia 89, 91
Carey, William 66
caste 12, 16, 17–19, 20, 21, 24, 35–7, 60, 62, 65, 66, 68, 71, 73, 74–87, 88, 92, 95, 100, 104, 105, 107, 109, 115, 116, 118
Chaitanya 27, 61, 63, 114
chandala 75–6, 118
  see also *dalit*; untouchables
Chandogya Upanishad 13, 25
Chatterjee, Debjani 44, 122
Chaudhuri, Nirad 8, 121
Christianity 1, 8, 63, 65–7, 68, 70, 78, 84, 103–4, 106
colonialism 62–74, 114–15
cow 52, 90, 100, 102–10

D

dalit 18, 19, 74–87, 108, 109, 116
  see also untouchables
darshana 24, 25, 50, 54, 55–9, 65, 111, 118
Dasharatha 40, 42
Dayananda Saraswati 67, 107, 114
Devi 43–6, 50, 51, 52, 55, 63, 68, 69, 118
Devi, Mataji Nirmala 98
Devi-mahatmya 45–6, 113
dharma 13, 17, 18, 34, 41–3, 46, 75, 79, 87, 88, 100, 102–10, 111, 118
diaspora 93, 97, 98, 99, 100
Divali 39, 58, 99, 118
dowry 44, 79–81, 115
Dravidian 5, 85, 104, 109, 118
Dubois, Abbé 65, 122
Durga 45, 51, 54, 59, 118
Durga Puja 54, 59, 99
Dutch 64, 92
dvaita vedanta 27, 30–1, 118

E

East Africa 89, 91, 92, 93, 97
East India Company 64, 66, 114
education 16, 20, 66, 83, 90, 91, 93, 97, 99, 104
  of women 66, 67, 78
Emerson, Ralph Waldo 70
Epics 12, 13, 29, 38–47, 118, 119

F

festivals 57–8, 92, 95, 97, 99
Flood, Gavin 125, 127, 128
French 64, 65, 72

G

Gandhi, Indira 74
Gandhi, Mohandas 35, 54, 71–2, 78, 82, 90, 107, 115, 122, 129
Ganesha 48–9, 53, 58, 61, 118
goddesses 13, 43–7, 49, 50, 51, 67, 78, 99, 103, 107
guru 10–22, 23–4, 27, 34, 53, 60, 62, 63, 68, 91, 96, 98, 99, 106
Guyana 89, 92, 94

H

Hanuman 41–2, 52
Harappa 5
Hare Krishna Movement, *see* International Society for Krishna Consciousness
Hastings, Warren 64–5, 114
hatha yoga 32, 35, 98
Hindu identity 36, 82, 83, 84, 85, 92, 98, 99, 105, 106, 107

Hindu migration 4, 88–101, 110, 113, 115
Hindu nationalism 3, 6, 35, 46, 47, 68, 78, 84, 107, 108, 109, 116
Hinduism:
  definitions 1–2, 102–10
  outside India 88–101
Hinduism Today 23, 100, 101, 121
hinduisms 102–10

I

icons 30, 49–51, 53, 105, 113, 119
idols, *see* icons
Indian National Congress 46, 70, 78, 115
Indus Valley civilization 5, 113
International Society for Krishna Consciousness (ISKCON) 23, 27, 28, 60–1, 97, 115
Internet 16, 23, 24, 81, 100
ishvara 29, 118
Islam 1, 62, 63, 66, 67, 84, 103, 106
Iyengar Yoga 98

J

Jaffrey, Madhur 43–4, 99, 122
Jainism 4, 106, 113
jati 18, 36, 75, 118
  see also caste
jnana yoga 34, 118
Jones, William 64, 65, 70, 114
Judaism 1, 103

K

Kabir 62–3, 76, 84, 114
Kaikeyi 40, 42
Kali 45–6, 52, 68, 92
Kanwar, Roop 73
karma 31, 32–7, 70, 109, 118
karma yoga 34–5, 71, 122
Katha 13
Klostermaier, Klaus 2, 125, 127
Krishna 9, 11, 13, 14, 30, 31, 34–5, 36, 37, 43, 50, 51, 52, 53, 55, 57, 58, 60, 61, 63, 68, 70, 118
kshatriya 18, 34, 42, 118

L

Lakshmana 38, 40–2, 52, 119
Lakshmi 45, 58
Laws of Manu, see *Manusmriti*
liberation 14, 19, 22, 28, 30, 32, 34, 35, 84, 111, 120
life-cycle rites 57, 95
linga 51, 60, 77, 118

M

Madhva 26, 27, 28, 30–1, 42, 114, 118
Madurai 59–60
Mahabharata 10, 13, 14, 29, 42, 43, 107, 113, 117, 118
Maitri 13
Malaysia 89, 91, 94
mandir, *see* temples
Manusmriti 13, 15, 36, 42, 76, 79, 87, 95, 107, 113, 118, 121, 122, 123
Markandeya Purana 13, 45
Mauritius 89, 91, 92, 94
Mirabai 76, 114
missionaries 50, 66, 70, 72, 84, 114
Mohenjo-daro 5
moksha, *see* liberation
Mughals 62, 63, 67, 104, 114
Muktananda, Swami 98
murti 30, 49, 50, 119
  see also icons
Muslims 38, 47, 62, 63, 79, 88, 91, 107, 109

N

Naidu, Sarojini 78, 115, 123
Nammalvar 15
Narayan, Ravana K. 11, 15, 19, 20, 121

Narayanan, K. R. 74, 116
Nepal 14, 88, 94
Netherlands 89, 95

O

Olcott, Colonel H. S. 70
orientalists 6, 7–8, 65, 67, 70, 104, 108, 128
Osho, *see* Rajneesh

P

Patel, Neerav 83, 123
Peggs, James 72
polytheism 8, 66, 68
Portuguese 64, 114
Pramukh Swami Maharaj 96
puja 51, 60, 95, 99, 119, 128
Puranas 10, 12, 13, 29, 51, 53, 113

R

Radha 11, 51, 52, 119
Radhakrishnan, Sarvepalli 104, 123
raja yoga 35
Rajneesh 98
Rama 11, 13, 38–45, 46–7, 51, 42, 58–9, 62, 85, 109, 119, 127
Ramabai, Pandita 78, 81, 114
Ramakrishna 68–9, 114
Ramakrishna Mission 69, 115
Ramakrishna Order 27, 69, 115
Ramanuja 7, 26–31, 32, 50, 97, 114, 119, 120, 126
Ramayana 10, 13, 14, 29, 39–43, 44, 51, 58–9, 85, 91, 92, 106, 113, 119, 127
Rambachan, Anantanand 2, 125, 127, 128
Ravana 38, 40–1, 43, 44, 59, 85
Ravidas 76, 85
reform 8, 65–7, 69, 70–2, 73, 76, 78, 81, 85, 105, 107, 108, 128
religion, definition of 1–2, 102–10, 130
religious transmission 10–22, 24
Rig Veda 4, 8, 12, 13, 14, 16, 18, 35, 119, 121
Roy, Ram Mohan 8, 66–7, 68, 73, 114

S

Sahaja Yoga 98
Sai Baba Movement 97
Sama Veda 13
samadhi 35
sampradaya 11, 27, 28, 96, 97, 99, 119
samsara 19, 32–7, 119
samskara, *see* life-cycle rites
sanatana dharma 3, 108
sannyasa 18, 95, 119
Sarada Devi 68–9, 85, 115
sati 8, 53, 66, 72–3, 79, 86, 114, 119, 128
self 21, 22, 23–37, 50, 53, 98, 111, 117, 120
Self-Realization Fellowship 98
Sen, K. C. 2
Shaiva Siddhanta Movement 23, 24, 31, 97, 115, 127
Shaivism 105, 113
Shaktism 105, 113
Shakti 45, 119
Shankara 7, 11, 21, 26–31, 32, 114, 117, 119, 126
Shankara-acharya 110–12, 20, 31, 57, 69, 74, 87, 119
Sharma, Arvind 35–7, 109, 122, 125
Shiva 5, 9, 13, 14, 31, 44, 45, 48, 50, 51–2, 58, 60, 63, 77, 118, 119
Shiva Purana 13
shruti 3, 12–15, 119
shudra 18, 119
Shvetashvatara 13
Siddha Yoga 35, 98
Sikhism 4, 84

Sita 11, 38, 40–5, 52, 71, 119, 127
Sivaya Subramuniyaswami 23
Smith, Brian K. 15, 121
smriti 12–15, 119
South Africa 69, 89, 92, 94
South-East Asia 40, 91, 95, 113
Sri Mata Amritanandamayi movement 23, 24, 27, 97, 115, 127
stri-dharma 17, 42, 78–9
Surinam 92, 94
Sutras 12, 13, 113
suttee, see *sati*
Swaminarayan Hindu Mission 23, 96–7, 116, 127
Swaminarayan Movement 27, 28, 114

T

tantra 14, 15, 31, 68, 84, 113
television 38, 39, 47
temples 49–51, 59, 61, 83, 92, 95–6, 97, 99, 130
  in Ayodhya 46–7, 109
  in Madurai 59–60
  in Vrindaban 51
  outside India 92, 95–6, 97, 99, 130
Thailand 89, 91, 95
Theosophical Society 70, 115
Thoreau, Henry David 70
Tilak, Bal Gangadhar 35, 122
Transcendental Meditation (TM) 98
Trinidad 92–3, 94, 123
Tulsidas 44

U

United States 40, 60, 69, 70, 71, 89, 93, 94, 97, 115, 126, 128, 130
untouchability 19, 71, 82–7, 115
untouchables 19, 66, 76, 81–2, 84, 87, 108, 129
Upanishads 12, 13, 16, 22, 24–6, 32, 51, 54–5, 67, 70, 113, 117

V

Vaishnavism 77, 105, 113
Valmiki 40, 41, 42, 43, 44, 85
varna 16, 18, 42, 71, 75, 118, 119, 120
varna-ashrama-dharma 17, 18, 42, 120
Vasco da Gama 64, 114
Vayu Purana 13
Veda 3, 4, 7, 8, 10–18, 24, 29, 75, 76, 79, 105, 119, 120
vedanta 13, 25–31, 70, 106, 111, 117, 118, 120, 126
  see also *advaita vedanta*; *dvaita vedanta*; *vishishtadvaita vedanta*
Vedanta Society 27, 69, 97, 115
Vedanta-sutra, see *Brahma-sutra*
Vertovec, Steven 92, 123
vishishtadvaita vedanta 27
Vishnu 13, 14, 29, 31, 43, 45, 50, 51, 52, 63, 117, 118, 119, 120
Vishnu Purana 13
Vishwa Hindu Parishad (VHP) 99
Vivekananda 26, 27, 68, 69–70, 97, 114, 121

W

Whitman, Walt 70, 122
Wilberforce, William 66
Wilkins, Charles 64, 65, 114
Wilson, H. H. 8
women 3, 17, 18, 35, 42, 44, 45, 53, 62, 66, 67, 69, 71, 73, 74–81, 85, 86, 87, 91, 95, 99, 100, 107, 108, 109, 115, 116, 123
  education 66, 67, 71
  and protest 74–81, 115, 123
women's movement 76–9, 84, 108
World Parliament of Religions 69, 115

worship 5, 8, 14, 30, 31, 48–60, 61, 67, 68, 77, 95, 96, 98, 99, 119, 123, 128

Y

yajna 17, 92, 95, 120
Yajur Veda 13
yoga 13, 25, 32–7, 85, 98, 111, 120, 122, 127
see also *bhakti yoga*; *hatha yoga*; Iyengar Yoga; *karma yoga*; Sahaja Yoga; Siddha Yoga

Expand your collection of VERY SHORT INTRODUCTIONS

1. Classics
2. Music
3. Buddhism
4. Literary Theory
5. Hinduism
6. Psychology
7. Islam
8. Politics
9. Theology
10. Archaeology
11. Judaism
12. Sociology
13. The Koran
14. The Bible
15. Social and Cultural Anthropology
16. History
17. Roman Britain
18. The Anglo-Saxon Age
19. Medieval Britain
20. The Tudors
21. Stuart Britain
22. Eighteenth-Century Britain
23. Nineteenth-Century Britain
24. Twentieth-Century Britain
25. Heidegger
26. Ancient Philosophy
27. Socrates
28. Marx
29. Logic
30. Descartes
31. Machiavelli
32. Aristotle
33. Hume
34. Nietzsche
35. Darwin
36. The European Union
37. Gandhi
38. Augustine
39. Intelligence
40. Jung
41. Buddha
42. Paul
43. Continental Philosophy
44. Galileo
45. Freud
46. Wittgenstein
47. Indian Philosophy
48. Rousseau
49. Hegel
50. Kant
51. Cosmology
52. Drugs
53. Russian Literature
54. The French Revolution
55. Philosophy
56. Barthes
57. Animal Rights
58. Kierkegaard
59. Russell
60. William Shakespeare
61. Clausewitz
62. Schopenhauer
63. The Russian Revolution
64. Hobbes
65. World Music
66. Mathematics
67. Philosophy of Science
68. Cryptography
69. Quantum Theory
70. Spinoza
71. Choice Theory
72. Architecture
73. Poststructuralism
74. Postmodernism
75. Democracy

76. Empire
77. Fascism
78. Terrorism
79. Plato
80. Ethics
81. Emotion
82. Northern Ireland
83. Art Theory
84. Locke
85. Modern Ireland
86. Globalization
87. The Cold War
88. The History of Astronomy
89. Schizophrenia
90. The Earth
91. Engels
92. British Politics
93. Linguistics
94. The Celts
95. Ideology
96. Prehistory
97. Political Philosophy
98. Postcolonialism
99. Atheism
100. Evolution
101. Molecules
102. Art History
103. Presocratic Philosophy
104. The Elements
105. Dada and Surrealism
106. Egyptian Myth
107. Christian Art
108. Capitalism
109. Particle Physics
110. Free Will
111. Myth
112. Ancient Egypt
113. Hieroglyphs
114. Medical Ethics
115. Kafka
116. Anarchism
117. Ancient Warfare
118. Global Warming
119. Christianity
120. Modern Art
121. Consciousness
122. Foucault
123. The Spanish Civil War
124. The Marquis de Sade
125. Habermas
126. Socialism
127. Dreaming
128. Dinosaurs
129. Renaissance Art
130. Buddhist Ethics
131. Tragedy
132. Sikhism
133. The History of Time
134. Nationalism
135. The World Trade Organization
136. Design
137. The Vikings
138. Fossils
139. Journalism
140. The Crusades
141. Feminism
142. Human Evolution
143. The Dead Sea Scrolls
144. The Brain
145. Global Catastrophes
146. Contemporary Art
147. Philosophy of Law
148. The Renaissance
149. Anglicanism
150. The Roman Empire
151. Photography
152. Psychiatry
153. Existentialism
154. The First World War
155. Fundamentalism
156. Economics
157. International Migration
158. Newton
159. Chaos
160. African History

161. Racism
162. Kabbalah
163. Human Rights
164. International Relations
165. The American Presidency
166. The Great Depression and The New Deal
167. Classical Mythology
168. The New Testament as Literature
169. American Political Parties and Elections
170. Bestsellers
171. Geopolitics
172. Antisemitism
173. Game Theory
174. HIV/AIDS
175. Documentary Film
176. Modern China
177. The Quakers
178. German Literature
179. Nuclear Weapons
180. Law
181. The Old Testament
182. Galaxies
183. Mormonism
184. Religion in America
185. Geography
186. The Meaning of Life
187. Sexuality
188. Nelson Mandela
189. Science and Religion
190. Relativity
191. The History of Medicine
192. Citizenship
193. The History of Life
194. Memory
195. Autism
196. Statistics
197. Scotland
198. Catholicism
199. The United Nations
200. Free Speech
201. The Apocryphal Gospels
202. Modern Japan
203. Lincoln
204. Superconductivity
205. Nothing
206. Biography
207. The Soviet Union
208. Writing and Script
209. Communism
210. Fashion
211. Forensic Science
212. Puritanism
213. The Reformation
214. Thomas Aquinas
215. Deserts
216. The Norman Conquest
217. Biblical Archaeology
218. The Reagan Revolution
219. The Book of Mormon
220. Islamic History
221. Privacy
222. Neoliberalism
223. Progressivism
224. Epidemiology
225. Information
226. The Laws of Thermodynamics
227. Innovation
228. Witchcraft
229. The New Testament
230. French Literature
231. Film Music
232. Druids
233. German Philosophy
234. Advertising
235. Forensic Psychology
236. Modernism
237. Leadership
238. Christian Ethics
239. Tocqueville
240. Landscapes and Geomorphology

241. Spanish Literature
242. Diplomacy
243. North American Indians
244. The U.S. Congress
245. Romanticism
246. Utopianism
247. The Blues
248. Keynes
249. English Literature
250. Agnosticism
251. Aristocracy
252. Martin Luther
253. Michael Faraday
254. Planets
255. Pentecostalism
256. Humanism
257. Folk Music
258. Late Antiquity
259. Genius
260. Numbers
261. Muhammad
262. Beauty
263. Critical Theory
264. Organizations
265. Early Music
266. The Scientific Revolution
267. Cancer
268. Nuclear Power
269. Paganism
270. Risk
271. Science Fiction
272. Herodotus
273. Conscience
274. American Immigration
275. Jesus
276. Viruses
277. Protestantism
278. Derrida
279. Madness
280. Developmental Biology
281. Dictionaries
282. Global Economic History
283. Multiculturalism
284. Environmental Economics
285. The Cell
286. Ancient Greece
287. Angels
288. Children's Literature
289. The Periodic Table
290. Modern France
291. Reality
292. The Computer
293. The Animal Kingdom
294. Colonial Latin American Literature
295. Sleep
296. The Aztecs
297. The Cultural Revolution
298. Modern Latin American Literature
299. Magic
300. Film
301. The Conquistadors
302. Chinese Literature
303. Stem Cells
304. Italian Literature
305. The History of Mathematics
306. The U.S. Supreme Court
307. Plague
308. Russian History
309. Engineering
310. Probability
311. Rivers
312. Plants
313. Anaesthesia
314. The Mongols
315. The Devil
316. Objectivity
317. Magnetism
318. Anxiety
319. Australia
320. Languages
321. Magna Carta
322. Stars
323. The Antarctic
324. Radioactivity

325. Trust
326. Metaphysics
327. The Roman Republic
328. Borders
329. The Gothic
330. Robotics
331. Civil Engineering
332. The Orchestra
333. Governance
334. American History
335. Networks
336. Spirituality
337. Work
338. Martyrdom
339. Colonial America
340. Rastafari
341. Comedy
342. The Avant-Garde
343. Thought
344. The Napoleonic Wars
345. Medical Law
346. Rhetoric
347. Education
348. Mao
349. The British Constitution
350. American Politics
351. The Silk Road
352. Bacteria
353. Symmetry
354. Marine Biology
355. The British Empire
356. The Trojan War
357. Malthus
358. Climate
359. The Palestinian-Israeli Conflict
360. Happiness
361. Diaspora
362. Contemporary Fiction
363. Modern War
364. The Beats
365. Sociolinguistics
366. Food
367. Fractals
368. Management
369. International Security
370. Astrobiology
371. Causation
372. Entrepreneurship
373. Tibetan Buddhism
374. The Ancient Near East
375. American Legal History
376. Ethnomusicology
377. African Religions
378. Humour
379. Family Law
380. The Ice Age
381. Revolutions
382. Classical Literature
383. Accounting
384. Teeth
385. Physical Chemistry
386. Microeconomics
387. Landscape Architecture
388. The Eye
389. The Etruscans
390. Nutrition
391. Coral Reefs
392. Complexity
393. Alexander the Great
394. Hormones
395. Confucianism
396. American Slavery
397. African American Religion
398. God
399. Genes
400. Knowledge
401. Structural Engineering
402. Theatre
403. Ancient Egyptian Art and Architecture
404. The Middle Ages
405. Materials
406. Minerals
407. Peace
408. Iran

409. World War II
410. Child Psychology
411. Sport
412. Exploration
413. Microbiology
414. Corporate Social Responsibility
415. Love
416. Psychotherapy
417. Chemistry
418. Human Anatomy
419. The American West
420. American Political History
421. Ritual
422. American Women's History
423. Dante
424. Ancient Assyria
425. Plate Tectonics
426. Corruption
427. Pilgrimage
428. Taxation
429. Crime Fiction
430. Microscopy
431. Forests
432. Social Work
433. Infectious Disease
434. Liberalism
435. Psychoanalysis
436. The American Revolution
437. Byzantium
438. Nuclear Physics
439. Social Psychology
440. Water
441. Criminal Justice
442. Medieval Literature
443. The Enlightenment
444. Mountains
445. Philosophy in the Islamic World
446. Light
447. Algebra
448. Hermeneutics
449. International Law
450. Moons
451. Sound
452. Epicureanism
453. Black Holes
454. The Body
455. Fungi
456. The History of Chemistry
457. Environmental Politics
458. Modern Drama
459. The Mexican Revolution
460. The Founding Fathers
461. Hollywood
462. Goethe
463. Medieval Philosophy
464. Earth System Science
465. Slang
466. Computer Science
467. Shakespeare's Comedies
468. The Welfare State